LETTERS TO MY

GRANDDAUGHTER

LETTERS TO MY GRANDDAUGHTER

A Grandmother's Gems Connecting Family, Community and Service

Eleanor Williams-Curry

iUniverse, Inc.
New York Lincoln Shanghai

Letters To My Granddaughter
A Grandmother's Gems Connecting Family, Community and Service

iUniverse books may be ordered through booksellers or by contacting:

iUniverse
2021 Pine Lake Road, Suite 100
Lincoln, NE 68512
www.iuniverse.com
1-800-Authors (1-800-288-4677)

Cover Design © Copyright 2006 William Curry and Laura Teal

Library of Congress

ISBN-13: 978-0-595-39513-2 (pbk)
ISBN-13: 978-0-595-83912-4 (ebk)
ISBN-10: 0-595-39513-9 (pbk)
ISBN-10: 0-595-83912-6 (ebk)

Printed in the United States of America

Contents

Foreword . . . . *xi*

Introduction . . . .*xv*

PART I   EARLY YEARS

Chapter 1   "What was life like for you growing up?" 3

Chapter 2   "Do you remember your first job? 19

Chapter 3   "Did you meet any celebrities as a
                young girl?" 26

Chapter 4   "When did you meet Papa Curry?" 29

Chapter 5   "How old were you when your mother
                died?" 34

Chapter 6   "What was it like falling in love?" 38

Chapter 7   "How did you survive eight kids?" 42

Chapter 8   "How did you stay sane raising eight
                children?" 46

Chapter 9   "Why is family important to you? 55

PART II   HOW OUR CHILDREN SAW IT

Chapter 10   Aunt Brenda 69

Aunt Bonnie 73

Aunt Barbara 77

Uncle Rich 80

Uncle Arnold 81

Dad 82

Uncle Paul 83

Uncle David 85

Chapter 11   Rewards of Giving 87

Chapter 12   The House that Love Built 90

PART III   VIPS

Chapter 13   "Have you met any celebrities?" 99

Chapter 14   Running with Ministers 130

Epilog *139*

Acknowledgments *141*

CURRY FAMILY TREE

First Generation

Richmond Earl Curry	Eleanor Williams
April 2, 1926	February 4, 1928
St. Louis, Missouri	St. Louis, Missouri

(Married 1946)

Second Generation

(Eight Children)

Brenda Rose

August 25, 1946

St. Louis, Missouri

Bonnie Rojeanna

September 14, 1947

St Louis, Missouri

Barbara Alice

October 6, 1948

St. Louis, Missouri

Richmond Earl, Jr.

October 31, 1951

St. Louis, Missouri

James Arnold

April 12, 1953

St. Louis, Missouri

William Howard

August 21, 1956

San Francisco, California

Paul Anthony

May 23, 1958

San Francisco, California

David Eric

May 18, 1960

San Francisco, California

Third Generation

(Twenty-three Grandchildren)

Brenda's children	Ava, John-John, Marla
Bonnie's children	Travis, TL, Jason
Barbara's children	Sterling, Eleanor, Michael
Richmond's children	Richmond Earl, III, Anthony, Ava
James' children	Marcella, Austin, Shannon, Nicholas
William's children	Justin, Danielle, Kyle
Paul's children	Lillian, Paul, Danny-Dan
David's child	Daric

Fourth Generation

(Sixteen Great-Grandchildren)

Ava's children	**Martel, Bianca**
Marla's child	Nijae
TL's children	Xavier, Bonnie-Jade
Jason's child	Princess
Sterling's children	Sterling, Jr., Christian, Alexis
Michael's children	Michael, Jr., Allen, Keith

Richmond Earl's, III children   Shaina, Quincy

Anthony's child   Miles

Marcella's child   Malcolm

Foreword

I have known my dear friend, Eleanor Williams-Curry, for many years. I am honored to write this introduction for an inspiring woman with such love for life and humanity. She is a community leader, a woman of vision and a person of action who is highly respected by others. Eleanor has many gifts to share and life lessons to teach us.

I was thrilled when I first heard she was writing a book. I knew that she had a wealth of wisdom. And it is fitting that Eleanor chose letters as her medium for sharing her life with her granddaughter and now us, for her letters dexterously reflect her values and strengths.

Eleanor has always valued family. She doesn't just say family is important, she lives it. Early on she knew the importance of keeping the family together and strong. Sometimes it even boiled down to the most basic things, like three square meals and simple structure. Yet many families cannot even provide that today. It doesn't have to be as complicated as we often make it. She proves this, showing that some of the most important things we need to give to our children are the less complicated. With eight children, 23 grandchildren and 16 great-grandchildren, Eleanor passes on her life lessons and personal history to the next generation. These letters remind us how our past can help our family and others prepare for the future only if we are willing to share it. We can have a stronger, healthier society when we know our history. Are you familiar with this expression? "You have to know where you've been to know where you are going."

Life long learning could be one of the most important practices that allow us to be open to new opportunities and see the world in a different light. I consider myself a life long learner. I believe it allows me to be a better person, a community member and a more effective policy leader, and I admire Eleanor's spirit of life long learning perseverance and how she applies it to her life. Her emphasis on the importance of education in school and throughout her life began with her childhood curiosity, as you will read in this book. As wise and strong as she inherently is, Eleanor seems never to miss an opportunity to learn and grow. As she shows, being open to learning can help prepare us for the bumps in the road along our journeys.

A desire to learn and a commitment to public service allow Eleanor to participate in numerous activities where she continues to make a difference. She is one of the most capable, compassionate and critically thinking people I know. Her two greatest public accomplishments which I'm familiar are co-founding the San Mateo County Commission on the Status of Women and creating the Curry Fund for Girls and Young Women. She created the latter by making caftans right in her home and selling them to raise the start-up money. Eleanor seems to make the most of every moment God has given her.

One of my favorite stories about her revolves around her initial meetings with a mutual friend. They decide to create the first San Mateo County Women's Hall of Fame book, entitled *Portraits of Dedication*, without any experience of the necessary steps, especially the cost. After a few coffee meetings, the friend asks Eleanor, "Why do we keep meeting at Nordstrom for coffee?"

Eleanor exclaims, "We have to think rich!"

They finished the book.

Eleanor always thinks big and outside of the box. She has great success in creating something out of nothing, because of her expectant outlook and process dedication.

I was not surprised, therefore, when she once said, "My eyes open habitually at 6:30 a.m. I shall never retire. I love life." Eleanor's humor and encouraging disposition is sprinkled throughout this book. This gives her the exorbitant energy that she has. However, she'll tell you that her faith keeps her going strong.

At the same time, her ability to give abundantly to others stems from her desire to see people reach their highest potential. She believes it is necessary to empower communities to do better for themselves and others. Eleanor's lesson about help is, "Whenever another person sees potential in you, if it's good advice, take it," a philosophy we share. Taking risks in order to make progress requires fearlessness, a characteristic I greatly admire in Eleanor.

Through this book Eleanor leaves a living legacy of giving, risking, thinking big, and one, too, of hope and love. Imagine if we all wrote letters to our grandchildren! What would our letters say? Surely, each would tell a unique story, one that our grandchildren would want to hear and should know. I hope you are as touched as I have been by her timeless stories.

Rose Jacobs Gibson
San Mateo County Board of Supervisors

Introduction

Letters to My Granddaughter is the result of one of my grandchildren, Danielle, asking me many questions about my life. Her questions began during a shopping trip shortly after Christmas of 1996. Although I had shared with my children stories about my early life, none of them had ever sought as much information about our family as did Danielle.

I promised her I would put answers to her questions in writing and give them to her in the form of letters. I fulfilled that promise by presenting her with the letters on her birthday the following year.

Since that time, both Danielle and I have shared the letters with countless family members and friends, all of who encouraged me to turn the letters into a book. That journey began in earnest in early 2003.

I found Danielle's questions extremely thought provoking. In an attempt to fully answer them, I have included much detail (more than she may have been expecting) with the hope of providing an insightful accounting of important events in my life.

PART I

▼

EARLY YEARS

CHAPTER 1

▼

"WHAT WAS LIFE LIKE FOR YOU GROWING UP?"

Dear Danielle,

I've spent a lot of time recalling my formative years. This period was so important to the remainder of one's life that we can almost label it the foundation for all of our tomorrows. Mine was full of protective love, unsuspected pain and spontaneous laughter. It shaped the woman am I today. I did pinpoint precise seconds during the ride 'back in the day' when living was so different for me. Your questions prompted me to recall incidents that I thought no longer relevant, buried deep into the furthest recesses of my mind. In these pages are some of the memorable events of my childhood.

Early Recollections

Aunt Sally, my mother's Aunt said to me when I was six years old, "You was born in a house. (February 4, 1928). Aunt Sally also grum-

3

bled, "Ophelia gone and had another baby. Lord knows why; and in the dead of winter!" Aunt Sally had long gray hair parted down the center. She mostly sat and rocked and mumbled to herself or her cats or the pigeons. She rarely talked to anyone in particular. But this day she wanted me to know where I was born. She kept talking, "No place for colored people 'over yonder'. Do you hear me child?" I nodded up and down. We were often told "Children are to be seen, not heard", so I dare not speak. 'Over yonder' was the "white side of town." There you'd find nice houses, stores, shops, restaurants and banks, the post office and even a hospital. People over yonder had everything they needed. While on our side of town, I saw a church, a drug store, the tavern, a grocery store, the school and the houses.

I arrived in the world in St. Louis, Missouri, the largest city along the Mason-Dixon Line. Prior to the Civil War, slavery was legal in Missouri and many other Southern states. The colloquialism Mason-Dixon Line came to be used as the unofficial dividing line between free Northern states and slave-held Southern states. Since Missouri had been a slave state, many of the racial prejudices customary at the turn of the century still existed long after slavery had been abolished. When I was growing up, St. Louis was separated by race concerning where people lived and sometimes worked.

My mother, Ophelia, was trained as a nurse. The segregation laws would not allow her to work in the white hospital. So instead of pursuing a career in her field of training, she married my dad, Roy Abraham Williams. She held odd jobs at the homes of wealthy white people. She served as a maid, cook, housekeeper and taking care of their children. Mother stood only four feet, eleven inches tall, had caramel colored skin and shoulder length hair. Daddy looked just the opposite at six feet with jet-black skin and sharp chiseled features. Mother was a wise woman. She was extra good at figuring things out. She excelled at singing, reading, maintaining a cheerful attitude, and the ability to make others think. She loved Jesus with all her heart. She never allowed "bloody swearing" in her presence. She believed in the family being together, wanted her children to get an education and chastised us to be good so as not to embarrass the family. Even though we had very little material things, Mother always believed life would get better. She nursed the neighbors when they were sick. When she was fortunate enough to receive bits of meat and dry goods from the families whose houses she cleaned, she'd share food with our neighbors.

My maternal grandmother was entirely different Ophelia had married "down," which was the case any time a colored person married someone darker than one's self. My grandmother constantly complained to anyone who would listen. Skin color was everything, during this period in American history. Society's racial pulse was deeply ingrained in young and old alike. Children readily accepted the status quo, even going so far as to recite this rhyme while jumping rope: *If you're white, you are right/If you're yellow, you are mellow/If you're brown, stick around/If you're black, get back.*

There were few attempts to instill racial pride in the hearts and minds of black people. Back then, if you were black you were just that—black. As a race we were called either colored or Negro. There was no "African American" or "Black" or any other racial term that gave you a sense of dignity about yourself. You were just colored, period. My grandmother hated Roy because of his darkness. I can still hear her saying, "Ophelia's hard headed. She married a man beneath herself. He's too dark to amount to anything." Ophelia and Roy had six children (Lois Mae, Clifford, Charles, Roy, Eleanor {that's me}, and Earl. We realized we were a beautiful assortment of skin tones. However, back then we were just colored children. My mother's family was seen as colored aristocrats. They had light skin, were highly intelligent and owned a house. Few colored people owned houses. My grandmother's station in life did not help us during hard times. Everything that happened to us was my mother's fault for marrying a dark man, in her eyes.

My Daddy died when I was four years old. One day, mother had to return to her mother's house with all of us kids to live. She could no longer afford the rent. Actually we moved to grandmother's basement. The day we arrived I bounded up the porch steps to the front door because I needed to go to the bathroom. Naturally I headed to the front door because it was the closest. I can still feel the heat of that warm summer day. Before I even knocked, grandmother opened the door and gave me a stern look.

"Where do you think you're going?" She asked me in a chilled voice.

"I have to go to the bathroom." I said anxious.

"Never come to this front door again. Do you understand me?"

"Yes Ma'am."

"The back door is for darkies. Make sure you use it."

"Yes Ma'am."

I had to run all the way around to the back of her house that time. That's the only conversation I remember having with my grandmother. She always looked at us as though we were the lowest people on earth. Personally, I mostly avoided her staying out of her way.

But mother had a way of making the best out of every situation. All of us kids helped carry our few meager belongings to grandmother's basement, except our mattresses. We didn't take them to the basement because Mother cheerfully said, "Hey kids! I've got a surprise for you." Of course we jumped around her in anticipation, shouting at mother all at the same time.

"Is it candy? Do we get new toy? Mother, mother, please tell us what's the surprise!"

"Tonight we are going to sleep under the stars," she said.

"We are? How can we do that?"

"We're going to place our mattresses in the backyard and build tents with our blankets. Now come on. Let's get ready before dark."

Clifford, Charles and Roy ran to the curb to unload the mattresses from the neighbor's truck. Lois Mae grabbed blankets from the truck.

"Mother, what can I do?" I joyfully asked.

"Why don't you help me put the sheets on?"

After the boys laid out our few tattered mattresses, we put sheets on and propped up our blankets with boxes and sticks, whatever we could find to render the blankets a few feet above our "beds." Thanks for the St. Louis summer heat. We spent most of the summer sleeping "under the stars."

Looking, Listening, Learning

Children hear tons of comments from an early age that does not make sense because no one explains anything to them. I caught a lot about life by listening, usually behind a closed door, standing near an open window, peeping through a keyhole, or sitting on someone's lap. While the old folks "signified" about things people had done, I often wondered what they meant. These adult conversations were usually interspersed with, "Lord only knows," or "Lord have mercy." One of my favorites was 'Every goodbye ain't gone. Every shut eye ain't sleep'. Later I'd repeat the phrase seeking an explanation I might understand.

Conversations I overheard from Lois Mae made me wonder about my daddy. *Where is my daddy? What is his name? Why doesn't he ever come home?* Some days my sister would come home from school and announce, "I'm going up to daddies."

"Can we go too?" Clifford would ask.

"No!" Lois Mae snapped. "I've to get some money. Ain't enough time to be watching y'all."

She'd leave, slamming the broken down screen door. Hours later she'd return, sometimes with money, sometimes without. Since no one ever talked to me about my daddy, I came to some conclusions on my own. His name was *Up-to-Daddies.* He lived on a job where he couldn't come home. He had to stay there all night and shovel coal in the furnace to keep the hotel rooms warm for the white people who lived there. He was working so he could give my sister this money. I wasn't quite sure what you were supposed to do with money, but it sure made Lois Mae happy. She would skip and smile when

Up-to-Daddies gave her money. She would be mean and angry when she couldn't get any.

Most of Lois Mae's anger would be directed at mother. They would go into the front bedroom and close the door. I'd ease up close to the bedroom door and listen to the shouting.

"He's your husband! Why can't he come home?"

"Child, you're too young to know," mother replied, barely audible.

"Make me know!"

"Keep your place," my mother emphatically whispered.

Then there was only silence from behind the closed door. I began to feel frightened and moved away just before the door opened. I felt frustration because I had not gotten any answers about Up-to-Daddies.

As I got older, I found that I had been right about Daddy's works that happen 'over yonder'.

Close Relatives

I remember other relatives emerging around the time when I was four years old. There was Uncle "King" Bob who worked at the ice packing house, Uncle Cecil who loved to play the saxophone at the night club, and Uncle Woody who sometimes watched us in the winter when mother worked late. Of all the relatives, Aunt Sally was the strangest person. I can still see her standing on the sidewalk talking to the pigeons. They'd flock around her gobbling down breadcrumbs she had tossed. At first I thought she just liked the pigeons. Then one day Lois Mae said to us, "Y'all better not eat that soup Aunt Sally been making. She's got pigeons in it."

"What you say?" Clifford asked in amazement.

"She's putting the pigeons in her soup. She wrings their necks just like you do a chicken, plucks the feathers off, cuts them up and puts them in the soup pot."

"Oh no," moaned Charles.

"Y'all better not eat that soup. Pigeons are really dirty birds so don't eat it."

After that day no matter how hungry we were, we never ate Aunt Sally's Dirty Bird Soup.

I recall the day my daddy died as though it were yesterday. It was a warm October afternoon. Yellow, orange and brown leaves had fallen from nearby trees. I was walking back and forth, crushing the leaves beneath my feet just like many a four-year-old child has done. Lois Mae suddenly ran up the street crying and hollering, "Mother! Mother!" She bolted up the wooden steps to our front door faster than anything I'd ever seen. Mother flung open the door and demanded, "What happened?"

"It's Daddy!"

Mother grabbed Lois by the shoulders in an attempt to calm her down.

"Lois, what is it? What happened?"

"He's gone," Lois Mae sobbed.

Mother and Lois Mae stood there hugging each other. They both were silent. No one noticed me. I wondered where my daddy had "gone."

Over the next three days, people came to our house from everywhere. They brought flowers, baskets of fruit, fried chicken wrapped in checkerboard cloth and homemade cakes and jars of jelly to spread on homemade bread. The white family mother worked for came over in a long black car. They hugged my mother, told us kids hello, and left. I was overjoyed from all those people coming over and bringing us so much food.

On day five after my daddy had "gone," we all got up and put on the clothes usually reserved for Sunday; what we called our Sunday-go-to-meeting clothes. Somehow I knew it was only Saturday, not the day for church. But I still felt happy to be all dressed up and ready to go someplace. So there I was all dressed up, prancing around and singing when Clifford said to me, "Stop prancing around. You're givin' the wrong impression."

"What's impression?"

"Just shut up and watch," Clifford said.

So that's what I did. I watched as Uncle Cecil, the saxophone player, arrived in his Model-T automobile. He was the only one who had a car. Uncle Cecil seldom took us out. There he was in his Sunday-go-to-meeting clothes too. He helped mother and me get into his car. I got to ride with mother because I was the smallest. We stopped at the church, went inside and took our seats. It was very quiet. I was looking around. The preacher went to the front of the church and started talking.

Soon after, I remember walking up to the front of the church to look at my daddy lying in a long wooden box. I asked my mother, "Is daddy sleep?" I got no answer. I also remember getting a lot of attention that day. I do not remember hearing anyone saying the words 'death' or 'died.' After that day, Lois Mae never went Up-to-Daddies any more. Somehow my little brain figured out that 'gone' did in fact mean really gone.

Kindergarten for a Day

I started kindergarten in 1934 at age six. The previous year mother had told me, "Eleanor, I'm going to keep you home with me so I can teach you how to read." As my sister and brothers headed off to school that year, mother set about writing the word for everything in our house on a piece of white paper. She then taped each word to the object it identified. Items like icebox, table, chair, stove, door, window, floor, curtain, sink, etc., all got identifying labels so I could read them. Mother also invented a game for me called the Word Families. She'd say, "Okay, today we're going to learn about the 'at' family." She'd write all the words she could think of containing the "at" sound: cat, bat, rat, sat, mat, hat, fat, etc. Then we'd say the words together. I can still remember my amazement at seeing how many words were in the "at" family. Together we studied the sounds of many other word families until I could read just about any word that was put in front of me. The entire process was so much fun that I didn't see it as work. I was learning how to read and loved every moment of it. On the first day of school, the teacher pinned a note on my blouse for my mother to read. I took the note off and began, "Dear Mrs. Williams, Please come over to the school tomorrow." I continued reading the entire note. The teacher looked surprised and asked me to come to the front of the class. She picked up a book from her desk and asked me if I could read it. I read an entire page, then another.

"Who taught you how to read?"

"My mother," I said proudly.

"Tell your mother to bring you to school in the morning."

I did. She came. That same day they put me in first grade. The real reason Mother had kept me home that year (according to Lois Mae) was because, "She can't afford to buy you any shoes." But who cared? I sure didn't. Besides, I could now read.

The Green Dress

I'm now in the third grade with the Christmas break upon us. . . That Christmas the Welfare Department sent out clothing for every child of school age needing assistance. Mother was still struggling as a maid. It was awful. We only had money for food and the barest of necessities. We ate a lot of cooked greens and hot water cornbread. We drank a lot of water. Mother caught fish from a nearby lake during the summertime. It was now a brisk cold winter day. Christmas was only a week away. Lois Mae and I received a green dress with white pockets on the front and a big green bow tied at the back of the waist. I thought it was beautiful and didn't wear it at all during the Christmas break. I wanted to save it for school. The night before school I couldn't sleep. I was too excited about showing up in school the next day in my new dress. Lois Mae saw it differently. "You're so silly," she said to me. "It's just a dress. Nobody at school cares one bit about it."

"When they see how good I look they will."

"No they won't. You need your head examined. Nobody cares."

"You'll see. Just wait."

The next day I was the first one out of bed. I walked the short distance to the school with Lois Mae. As soon as we turned the corner I heard loud laughter. When I looked toward the sound of the laughter, a group of girls pointed at me, falling out laughing and yelling, "Hey, look! Here comes another one of those welfare dresses." I quickly scanned the schoolyard. I was amazed when I saw several other girls with a green dress on just like mine. Seeing the other dresses didn't bother me nearly as much as the jeering from the crowd of girls who were wearing their own clothes. Tears filled my eyes, nearly blinding me as I turned and ran.

"Eleanor, Eleanor, come back!" Lois Mae called. Where are you going?"

I didn't even turn around to answer her. I was too embarrassed to look back.

"Eleanor, stop! You're going to get hit by a car if you don't look where you're going."

I didn't stop. Lois Mae finally caught up with me and said, "You shouldn't worry about what other people think. They're stupid anyway. You're crazy for letting them get next to you."

When I burst through the door of our house, mother asked me, "What's wrong, baby?"

Through my tears and runny nose I responded, "They laughed at me, mother. A group of girls were standing outside the school waiting for anyone wearing a green dress. They pointed their fingers at me and said 'we were too poor for you to buy me any real clothes."

"She is too poor. You need to stop sheltering that girl, mother," Lois Mae said. "It's a cold world out there. Here she's crying about what some stupid girls said."

"That's enough, Lois Mae. Leave her be."

"That green dress looks better than most of the rags we usually wear. You need to grow up girl."

"I said that's enough, Lois Mae."

In her usual easy going way, mother said to me, "Go wash your face and take the dress off, Eleanor." I took the dress off and threw it on the floor. I never wanted to see that green dress again. But mother wasn't done. She looked at me and quietly said, "They're never laugh at you again. I'm going to teach you how to sew."

Mother and I made most of my school clothes, from that day until she died. Now of course there was no money to buy cloth for new clothes. So after the green dress disaster, mother showed me how to carefully take apart the seams of any clothes using a razor blade. We'd then re-cut the fabric into pieces for a skirt or, blouse and hand-sew the new item together. I thoroughly enjoyed the times I spent sewing with Mother. She was right. The kids never laughed at me again.

My Eye Operation

The segregation laws of the day were a real drag. But for the grace of God and an understanding white doctor, I easily could have lost sight in my left eye. One day when I was seven years old, I was glazed on my left temple by a baseball bat when my brothers were playing baseball. Since I wasn't knocked down or bleeding, none of us kids thought much of it. But the next morning Mother noticed that my left eye didn't look quite right. The pupil, without any help from me, had shifted to the left side of my eye socket. Mother took me to the hospital. They examined both eyes and informed her that I needed an operation. They told her that they could not perform the surgery because this was a "segregated facility." Mother took me home. My condition didn't improve. When I asked mother how I was going to get my surgery, she told we would have to "pray on it." When the eye showed no signs of improvement, we returned to the hospital. This time there was a white doctor on duty. He was from one of the Northern States. He told the staff that I was just a child. He was going to operate on my eye, or he would leave the facility. So that's how I got my eye surgery.

The biggest miracle beyond the eye surgery was when I discovered how much Miss De Lancey, my fourth grade teacher liked me. When

I returned to school with a big white patch covering my left eye, many of the students crowded around me poking at me and laughing about the patch. I was terrified. She came outside to the play yard and rescued me. She explained once, in class we are to help, not hurt people when something happens to them. Guess what else happen? While different students decided to help me catch up with the reading assignments I had missed, Miss De Lancey took a special interest in the book reports I had to prepare for our class. One day she told me, "Eleanor you will become somebody good for our people. You could even be a great writer." Of course I did not have a faintest idea what she was telling me. Can you believe some forty years later I met her again? We were in East Palo Alto, California. I was the Guest Speaker. I talked about the value of one significant person being in a child's life. Such a person can guide any child in the right direction, regardless of who they are, where they live or what they need. I was telling the audience about my fourth grade teacher. I finished my presentation. My fourth grade teacher came to the stage. I was astonished to discover she was in California, too. We embraced and nearly cried tears of joy.

The Eureka Flats

The last place I lived with mother was the worst. It was called the Eureka Flats (the "Flats" for short). There were roughly twenty or thirty buildings in the Flats, four flats to a building, two up and two down. Each family had two rooms: a kitchen and an oversize bedroom. Each building had only one toilet and tub, so the four families in each building shared these facilities. At bath time, mother had to heat a bucket of water on the large black stove, and pour the water into a large number three tin tub. We had no electricity. Mother and I shared a big wooden bed in our lone bedroom. Our furniture was mismatched; an odd assortment of chairs and a table mother had managed to scrounge up. We also had an icebox (not to be confused with a refrigerator). An icebox had a long pipe inside to funnel water as the ice melted. A long drip pan was placed under the icebox to catch the water. The pan had to be emptied every night. If not, the next morning a puddle of cold water would be on the floor and you'd have to mop it up. There was an uncovered garbage dump out back. The rats lived there by day invisible to the human eye. They came looking for food in the Flats at night. We barely had enough food to feed ourselves, yet the rats thought otherwise. Your doors must always be locked at night from the rats. These were large grey creatures. If they managed to enter your rooms, a fight could pursue. If no food was available the rats might attempt to bite us. Boy was that a nightmare.

Somehow my mother managed to make this place as cheery as she could. She made curtains for the two windows in the place. A Christmas tree appeared each December. She'd decorate it with popcorn and cranberries strung together with thread. But of course it didn't light up. We did everything by candle or kerosene lamp (when we had money to buy the kerosene).

By the time we moved to the Flats, Lois Mae had grown up and married. Mother had told the three oldest boys to go and enlist in the Army. She could no longer afford to feed them. There were no jobs available for them either. Earl, my youngest brother, now thirteen years old, lived at the horse stables of a white family. He worked for them. Most of his pay covered room and board. So that left me living with mother in the Flats. I seldom saw my siblings any more. I was happy with mother though. She always believed things would get better. I prayed for her to be right.

My Teenage Years

Two weeks before the start of high school, I purchased my first pair of high-heel shoes—with two whole inches of heel. I eased into the right shoe, size ten. It fit. I knew the left shoe would fit because my right foot was slightly larger than my left. I was only thirteen at the time, yet I instantly felt taller and grown up. I looked in the shoe shop mirror, beginning at my feet, quickly glancing up to my face. Lipstick was forbidden until I turned fourteen. So I frowned at my plain reflection and at the prospect of having to wait. Quickly questions roamed around my brain. *Who am I? Do people like me? What am I good at? What can I really do? Am I special?* I paid for the shoes, walked out the door and caught the bus back to my side of town. As I've mentioned, everything in St. Louis was segregated. Colored people and white people lived, worked and attended schools on different sides of town. Although the city was segregated, it was seldom if ever discussed. I did know that I would be attending a high school for colored children only.

For a while when I was younger, my mother's friends and some of our neighbors affectionately called me 'Ophelia's baby girl.' The old man on the corner called me, "Ophelia's gal, you pretty little thing." Frowning, I ran past him fast, telling mother about his words. She laughed, saying to me that he was harmless. The teachers in school seemed to like me, too. I did my homework, getting good grades. I could hardly wait for high school. I hoped to make good grades there as well. But I had been forewarned about high school being hard. Right in my own family, my older sister, LoisMae had quit after the eighth grade. My next two brothers left at tenth grade and joined the Army. I wanted to find out for myself why school seemed so hard for them.

The final two weeks of summer finally ended. I entered Sumner High School. I was thrilled. The building looked like a castle. It took up a long city block on the Avenue. We walked up sixteen steps before entering the premises. We soon learned our school was named after Charles Sumner, a rich white man from the North who decided after the Civil War in the 1860s that colored children should have an education too. Danielle, I was impressed. I knew immediately high school was definitely for me.

After getting settled into all my classes and accustomed to the routine of high school, I discovered some great subjects. I was excelling in all my classes, including the school choir. I was the first girl at our high school to take an industrial arts class. This is the study of printing, drawing blueprints for houses and using a master cylinder to roll out the finished blueprint. Can you believe this? I was eager to take any subject that was considered out of the norm. I signed up for a study about birds. That's right—birds. Our class would go out for bird walks once a week at six-thirty in the morning. I especially loved the chirping sounds from the birds, which were bright red cardinals, bluebirds and strutting peacocks. It was fascinating to hear their sounds and view the places where they lived in Forest Park. We saw some of the nests they had made. We watched in awe when they disappeared as if by a clock before seven-thirty in the morning.

A year after entering high school, my life had expanded. I discovered gymnastics, joined the track team, played volleyball and was moved to the starting (first) string of the choir. The sports activities took place at school after our required subjects. But the choir gave me my first opportunity to travel away from St. Louis. All the choir members rode on big yellow buses to nearby cities. I had never been so far away from home. As we traveled from town to town, we sang and practiced our songs. I sang alto, which is a lower sound. The boys teased me for having a low-pitched voice. They laughed and imitated how they thought I sounded. Don't boys act silly? I pretended not to hear, ignoring them as best I could. Just imagine roughly forty choir participants riding a bus together, and over half of them were boys.

Danielle, most of my friends lived in bigger houses than I did, their families drove nice cars. I lived alone with my mother and we didn't have any car. We were barely existing. All the time it felt so bad to be broke. But even though we were poor, the girls from the middle income area were my best and closest friends...However, for the first time I felt slightly panicky about the lack of money. I wondered where I fit in the scheme of things and how I would pay for college. There was no such thing as an allowance for me. Mother simply didn't have any money beyond paying rent, paying a few bills and buying food for the two of us. I put college way out of mind. I needed money now.

I decided to earn money by doing homework for some of the football players. They paid me seventy-five cents to a dollar for every homework assignment I completed. I was making about nine dollars a week. But this caused me to be up late at night. When my mother realized I was doing more than my own homework, she made me stop. I wondered to myself why I had to quit. Mother explained, "Some money might have a rope attached and it's too hard to break." In spite of my sparse living conditions, I was actually very cheerful and essentially a happy teenager.

Love,
Mama Curry

CHAPTER 2

▼

"DO YOU REMEMBER YOUR FIRST JOB?

How much did you make?
What did you do?
Did slavery still exist?"

Dear Danielle,

When I turned fourteen years old, I knew money was still a problem for my mother. I decided that since I was strong and healthy, I would get me a job.

My best friend's name was Arlene. Like most teenagers, we talked about everything. Arlene's family was part of the middle class. Several of us (girls and boys) would go to her house on Friday nights where we'd dance in the large basement room her father had made just for recreation.

Arlene had very light skin and thick black curly hair. A gray streak over the left temple gave her an exotic look. She and I were the same age.

I came to her house early on this particular Friday. "Arlene" I whispered, "Are you by yourself?"

"Yeah," she looked quizzical. "What's the matter?"

"I have to get a job," I said, determined.

Arlene laughed saying, "You're kidding. You're not old enough. Who would hire you?"

"I can find a job at the tavern as a barmaid. I can look older than fourteen with more make-up." I was emphatic, yet also doubting myself.

"Did you ask your mother yet?" The doorbell rang. The rest of the group had arrived for a night of dancing.

"Don't tell anybody," I said in a low voice. Arlene nodded okay running to answer the door.

Suddenly I did not feel like dancing. I'd forgotten I'd have to tell mother. As smart as I was in doing school assignments, I had not thought this one through. The thought of facing mother about getting a job was chilling; like having a glass of cold lemonade on a cold winter afternoon. I headed home, rolling my options around in my mind as I walked. *No job, no money. I've had enough of not having any money.* Rapidly my courage about getting a job began to return. We must get more money and get out of that rat hole. We definitely needed more money. I knew the tavern wouldn't worry about my age. But I also knew mother wouldn't approve of this job. I waited until Saturday to get bold enough to tell her.

"I found a job. It's near the corner across the street from the drugstore." My temperature began rising.

"You mean in the tavern, right?" Mother asked sternly.

I was struck silent.

"Not there, baby!" She acted determined. "You're ready to work? I'll help you find a job. But not at any tavern." Since mother cleaned houses, I was sure she must have been thinking about the same line of work for me. I silently tried to figure out how I would tell her I would not be a maid.

Not long after that Saturday morning, mother told me she had found me a job. She had somehow managed to get one of the rich white ladies she cleaned house for to arrange for me to have a job. Much to my surprise, she had found me a job as a bus girl in one of the local restaurants on the other side of town.

"If your grades drop, the job goes," mother warned sharply.

"Yes, Ma'am," I said out loud. Inside I thought, *what's wrong with her? She knows we are flat broke.*

Of course, the threat concerning my grades was connected to a constant message I'd been hearing since I was eight years old: "Get a good education 'cause nobody can take it away from you. You have to be twice as smart as them white kids." This had always puzzled me because we seldom saw any white people, especially white kids. I wondered if the adults were a little *touched in the head.*

Just anticipating my new job made sleep impossible. After Sunday church service, mother gave me the seven 'don'ts' for this new beginning:

"Don't be late. Don't get in no stranger's car. Don't miss the bus. Don't tarry after work. Don't let anyone see where you hide your money. Don't ask how much you make. They'll tell you. Don't spend any of your money before you get it." But the one thing mother did not tell me sent me into shock.

First day on the job, I punched in at exactly four in the afternoon, my start time. I discovered everybody at the job was white! I was now fifteen years old and the only colored girl hired to bus tables in an all-white neighborhood. Mrs. Bergman, the restaurant manager, looked to be about mother's age. I stood in front of her, panic-stricken.

"You're Ophelia's daughter." She sounded in charge. I quietly gazed at her, waiting for the next comment. I had been trained not to speak around white people. "The less you say, the better off your day," was how mother had phrased it.

She looked me up and down, paused, than cheerfully said, "You'll do just fine." She reached out, touching me and turning me around.

My entire body stiffened. I was terrified. I had never been scrutinized in this manner by anyone white before.

"Are you okay?" She asked, now concerned.

"Just fine, Ma'am," I mumbled. I've got to relax, I thought, realizing how desperately I needed this job. "I'm ready to work. I learn fast. Do I start today?"

"Yes you can start working today, my child." She threw her head back, laughing. "For a minute I thought you had changed your mind."

"No Ma'am," I softly said, "I'm ready."

I followed Mrs. Bergman through a swinging door that led us into the biggest kitchen I'd ever seen. Huge silver pots and pans hung from the ceiling on large hooks. Oversize oblong tables were completely covered with every kind of food imaginable. A variety of platters held cooked meats, fish and poultry. The left side of the room had another table with containers of fresh vegetables and rows of baked potatoes stacked in clear smaller containers. Next were rows of dinner plates, each prepared with a serving of salad. I saw a rotating cabinet with individual swinging shelves that, when rotated, moved the dessert of choice directly to the waitress. Several waitresses were moving around. They were busy making sure their stations were ready, tables were properly set, and water pitchers were filled.

"Once my guests are seated," Mrs. Bergman explained, "we must not allow them to become impatient for their dinners." I nodded, glancing around and taking in all those new sights and aromas.

Then I saw her. The busiest, most cheerful looking Negro woman you could imagine. She was robust, with the smoothest chocolate brown complexion, a steady eye gaze and swift hand movements. She prepared the plates of food with the precision of a rope jumper. The sight of her brought me to a point of exuberance. What a relief to see I was not the only one in this place who looked like me.

I finished at eight that evening and caught the bus back to my side of town. The bus ran along the north border where I lived, not passing along our street. So I walked, skipped and ran the last three blocks to our two-room flat. I arrived home at exactly eight thirty-five in the evening. Mother was waiting on our steps, smiling. This set my time to always arrive home from work; any later and mother would worry.

"How was it?" She looked happy, hoping for a positive response.

"You didn't tell me almost everybody over there was white!" I blurted out.

"Can a brown cow eat green grass and produce white milk?" She put her hands on her hips, continuing emphatically, "Forget whose white, honey. Do your work the best you can so you can get paid."

So, Danielle, I became a bus girl. What did I do? I was a waitress's helper. I cleared the tables after each course of food was served, kept the water glasses filled, and remained pleasant. One week later I received my earnings: ten dollars plus tips from my assigned waitress. On rare occasions the bus girls would also receive tips from the guests we served. The tips were low, around four or five dollars weekly.

What did a bus girl do?

Arrive twenty-five minutes before four o'clock to put on the furnished uniform, which consisted of a bonnet to cover our hair, a white short sleeve blouse, a pink floral pinafore, a gathered skirt stopping at the bend of the knee, white socks and white nurse-type shoes. Report to her station. Fold napkins. Set each table with silverware, water glasses and candles. This had to be done before the restaurant opened. Once the shift began we had to pay strict attention to all that was going on and be ready to remove any dishes from the guests' table each time a course was completed. This was necessary to avoid a long wait between courses. This was an important point to master. We had to remove the dishes quickly and quietly from the left side of the guests. The process was especially vital on excessively crowded nights. All this work for ten dollars a week plus tips. No, Danielle, slavery did not exist in the 1940s. But sometimes it felt like a slave's day probably felt.

Just as mother had insisted, I continued studying in school while working at the restaurant. Academically, I was one of the top-ten students at school, making straight A's. After maintaining a 4.0 grade point average for two-and-a-half years, our principal, Mr. Brinkley, decided he might be able to get me a four-year scholarship. He called the State Board of Education in Missouri. A white man came from the Board who reviewed my entire school record. He interviewed my mother and set a date for the following Monday morning to meet with both mother and me. Monday came and I was too eager to get to school to wait for mother. I left the house early that morning without her. Once at school, I went to the principal's outer office and sat down to relax. I heard loud shouting coming from the principal's inner office. The conversation I overheard went like this:

"I'm telling you she is that smart," Mr. Brinkley was shouting emphatically. "I know she can handle college. She's not only academically ready, but she is emotionally balanced and good in sports. I know she can handle college."

"I disagree with you completely," the State Board man replied. "I was up the entire weekend reviewing every facet of her records. I must tell you, this is an aberration. It's a fluke."

"You're dead wrong." Mr. Brinkley sounded angry. "You have not presented one grain of evidence to support your findings."

I held my breath, stunned, as they talked about me. I sat there petrified.

"Here's the best damn reason of all." The State Board man sounded frustrated, rushing out these final words: "Her father was just a janitor before he died and her mother is just a lowly maid."

I was in shock. I ran out of the office and raced back home. When I saw mother ready to go to the nine o'clock meeting, I stared at her with the most determined look of utter disgust on my face.

"Mother, you don't have to go over there after all. I don't want to go to college."

"What happened?" mother was perplexed. "Are you all right?"

"Sure." I blurted rapidly. "I might not be college material. I think I'll do it later." I could feel the tears coming. "I have to get back to school. See you later." I never told mother what had happened earlier that morning. I felt she had been hurt enough in her life without having to further worry about me. Later that morning, Mr. Brinkley called me into his office. I was extremely calm. He tried to reassure me, not knowing I had overheard that crazy conversation. He recommended me for the school's Honor Society. This cast me in the same intellectual light as the 'better classes of students.

But you see, Danielle, despite the setbacks and thwarted opportunities I enjoyed this period in my life. I loved school and kept studying in spite of not getting the scholarship. Although it was a tremendous interference, I had to move on to whatever was next.

Love,
Mama Curry

CHAPTER 3

▼

"DID YOU MEET ANY CELEBRITIES AS A YOUNG GIRL?"

Dear Danielle,

The first celebrity I ever met actually came to our high school. The school was all abuzz one Friday. Katherine Dunham, an American dancer, choreographer and dance composer, was coming to our school. She was noted for her interpretations of dances performed by black people in the West Indies and the United States. She studied extensively dances that were popular in Jamaica. Miss Dunham worked as a dancer and choreographer in motion picture and stage musicals, in the late 1930's and early 40's. She had organized her own dance company, touring the United States and Europe performing ballets based on African and Caribbean ceremonial and folk dances. Eartha Kitt had launched her career under Miss Dunham in 1948. Eartha Kitt would go on to become a famous dancer, singer and actress.

Miss Dunham was scouting for young talent from the high schools in the St. Louis area. She was looking for girls who could not only dance but had stamina The only two schools where Negroes attended were Sumner High and Vashon High. One girl from each high school would be chosen to perform in Miss Dunham's dance company. Many of us competed for this one spot. The finalist had to complete 500 knee-bend exercises in addition to a popular dance of the day. I was qualified and easily completed the knee-bends. I danced the *jitterbug* swing dance. Did I win? Nope. I came in third place. I missed that opportunity. But I kept on *jitterbugging* and doing my tap dance routines. Miss Dunham exposed me to another world and it was an honor I have long remembered.

After meeting Miss Dunham, I pondered what I would do to take care of myself once I graduated from high school in two years. Money was nowhere in sight for college. But I believed college had to be more important than working in the restaurant. What's next? The main contacts outside of St. Louis came from *Ebony* magazine, *True Confessions* magazine and radio station KMOX. I decided to gather as much information as I could from these three sources. One day I lay sprawled across the floor in our back bedroom reading *Ebony*. The article that caught my attention was by Mary McCleod Bethune, founder of Bethune Cookman College. She had written her Last Will & Testament and it was published in the magazine. One message leapt out at me:

"I leave you racial dignity. We, as Negroes, must recognize that we are custodians as well as heirs of a great civilization…We must learn to share and mix with all men."

I read this part over several times: "must learn to share and mix with all men." Who is she talking about? Ninety-nine percent of the people around me were Negroes. Occasionally we saw the white landlord, the Chinese restaurant owner, or the Jewish grocery store owner. But what does she mean "share and mix?" Miss Dunham had spoken of "peoples of the world" when she came to our assembly. She must share and mix with different people, I thought. I had this desire to go beyond the colored side of town, branch out and meet people differ-ent from me. The only questions were, though, *when* would I do this and *how* would I do this.

Yes, Danielle, as a teenage girl, meeting a celebrity widened my vision. Yet, I had no idea how to go out into the world and meet my challenges head-on. So education was still number one.

Love you,
Mama Curry

CHAPTER 4

▼

"WHEN DID YOU MEET PAPA CURRY?"

Dear Danielle,

Your grandfather to be, Richmond Earl Curry, was captain of the Sumner High School football team. Guess what? Due to this prestigious position, everybody in the entire student body knew him, except me. I was on the track team. I wasn't familiar with the world of football.

It was late September, a perfectly beautiful sunny afternoon. I was circling the track field practicing my laps I wore a white T shirt and white pleated shorts, bobby socks and new tennis shoes. I was unaware that right across the field, Earl was practicing football with Ernest Hockaday, one of the linesmen and a neighbor of mine. Ernest was one of several guys who acted as protector of a group of girls when would go to the Light Opera in Forest Park. Ernest was a lot of fun, yet none of us dated him. He was just a good friend. Earl suddenly noticed me across the field.

"Who is that?" He asked with a keen interest.

"That's Eleanor Williams, man. But you can forget her," Ernest laughed with a voice of authority. "All she does is study, work and run track."

"I want to meet her," Earl persisted.

"Okay man," Ernest replied with a hopeless grin. "I'll introduce you. But I bet you ten bucks you won't get to first base with her."

"Deal," Earl said emphatically. "When I win, don't go near her. All right?"

"Hey, man," Ernest laughed. "This will be the easiest ten dollars I ever won. Let's go so I can collect my money. But you ought to know you're wasting your time. She doesn't date, man."

They both ran over to me. Hearing the pounding feet on the cinder track I turned to see who was coming.

"Hi, Eleanor. I have someone I'd like for you to meet. This is Richmond Earl Curry," Ernest said as he bowed and extended his hand toward Earl.

We both said, "Hello," then stood there in an awkward silence which seemed to last for hours.

"Nice meeting you," I finally said, smiling politely. "See you around." I continued running around the track.

Over the next several weeks, Earl popped up at the most unexpected times. One of my duties at school was that of hall monitor in the afternoons. If classes were in session, students were required to obtain an "excuse" if they were going to be in the hallways. So one day shortly after meeting him, Earl showed up in the hallway and said to me, "Well hello there, Eleanor. How are you today?"

"I'm fine. Do you have an excuse?"

"Oh! You're my excuse," he answered, half laughing.

"Earl Curry, you need an excuse to be out here. Where are you headed?"

"To see you," he said, smiling.

"Okay. Now you've seen me. So you'd better get back to class."

"I'm not done seeing you yet."

"Yes you are. If you don't want me to write you a detention slip, you'd better leave."

"But I just got here."

"Bye, Earl Curry. Please go now."

"Okay. But only because you said please."

He finally left, but in parting turned and said, "I'll be back."

The very next day he was back—again without an excuse.

I said, "Hi Earl. What can I do for you?"

"You can lend me a quarter. I promise I'll pay you back."

Now keep in mind, back then a quarter was worth about three dollars in terms of its buying power. But I gave him the quarter with the hope that he would then leave. He did. The next day he was back again and said, "Guess what? Your quarter turned into fifty cents." He handed me a fifty-cent piece then turned around and left. For months Earl would show up with no excuse, his crazy antics and a smile to penetrate my dreams.

Earl told me later he was appalled to find out I didn't know him. He said he decided right then and there (the day we first met) to marry me so I would never forget him. Less than six months later we were courting. We'd go to the movies, to dances, out to dinner, bowling, and to football games. I did not understand football, but I enjoyed being with Earl.

We discovered we were both working after school. He worked on Saturdays too. Earl had a part-time job at the ice plant. He used ice tongs to haul huge blocks of ice into delivery trucks. Next he used an ice pick to break the ice blocks into smaller pieces. He rode in the ice-truck along with the driver. They'd sell the ice blocks throughout the neighborhood where families would place it in the iceboxes to keep perishable food from spoiling.

The more we found time to be with each other, the better I liked him. One rainy summer night, Earl took me to the Light Opera. After it ended, Earl walked me home. We were so enchanted with each other we didn't realize it was raining, first a slow drizzle than a steady warm stream. The two of us got soaked.

A few weeks later we went to the movies. One of mother's cardinal rules was, "Be home before midnight." Normally we'd ride the street-car home. That particular starlit night was perfect for a stroll. We decided to walk to my house—slowly. We lost all track of time. Together we sang a popular song of the day. The lyrics were so in tune with what we both were feeling. How does one explain love and always wanting the other person with you? We were both overcome with happiness.

We strolled along, singing, telling funny stories, holding hands and laughing, us together, oblivious to our surroundings. What was time at a moment like that? The closer we got to my house, I suddenly felt thrust into reality. I saw mother's reflection on the darkened porch, her head silhouetted against the light. When Earl saw mother standing on the porch, he stopped.

"Eleanor," he whispered, "I think your mother is upset."

"What time is it?" I quickly responded.

"I don't know," Earl said. "I'll wait here 'til you get to the porch. I'm afraid she won't let me see you anymore if I go up there right now."

I calmly moved toward the porch alone in the dark. Earl hid behind the bushes. Suddenly the stillness was broken.

"Come on up here Earl," mother's voice shouted out. "I want to tell both of you something."

Earl reluctantly came out of the bushes. Mother told us to come on in the house.

"Never bring Eleanor home after midnight. Is that clear?" mother said precisely.

We both nodded shamefully.

"Mrs. Williams, I'm so sorry," Earl apologized. "We lost track of time. I promise you this won't ever happen again."

"It better not," mother said. "You can go now, Earl."

"Yes, Mrs. Williams. Good night, Mrs. Williams." Earl turned and left.

"Sorry mother," I said sincerely. "Can I go to bed now?"

"Where else would you go?" mother asked. "Say your prayers."
Needless to say, it never happened again.

Danielle, the rest of our time together convinced us we were in love. Our school days were happy ones. We studied hard, kept our grades up and continued to work part-time. Earl was a senior and had been accepted at Kentucky State College. At the end of summer, he would be leaving. We were enjoying being together more and more. I couldn't imagine what I'd do once he left for college. I certainly was not prepared for the next set of circumstances and how fast my life would change.

Hugs & a big kiss,
Mama Curry

CHAPTER 5

▼

"HOW OLD WERE YOU WHEN YOUR MOTHER DIED?"

Dear Danielle,

I was 16 years old this past February 4th. Mother had not been feeling well for several months, though she seldom complained. I have no idea how sick mother really was. Earl was away at Kentucky State College. I was a senior in high School, just living one day at a time.

Mother was extremely quiet this particular morning. She appeared listless. I questioned her about how she was feeling. She told me not to worry. I promised to be home early from school. I left around seven-thirty to catch the bus. Around noon I began having strange sensations that left me feeling something was wrong. I wasn't exactly sure what it was. I felt hot all over, and then a chill made me shudder. Mother flashed across my mind. She had been ill for a while. Lately she had barely eaten any solid food. I didn't know why her appetite had left her.

Ring! Ring! Ring! Class was dismissed. We moved through the cluttered hallways of Sumner High. I was in a crowd of about a dozen of my friends all headed to Rosie's Hamburger Stand. This was a daily ritual for our group. Rosie's was about two blocks from White Castle Hamburgers on King's Highway Boulevard. White Castle, like many other stores, was still segregated, so it was natural to go to Rosie's.

I was a sharp dresser in high school, what you might call a 'clothes pace setter.' On this day I looked great in my swanky maroon short skirt, a starched long sleeve white cotton shirt, spanking white bobby socks and gleaming white tennis shoes. Yet, that feeling of anxiousness would not leave me. I slowly walked toward Rosie's. Half a block away my head started throbbing. My heart was pounding like a drum roll. *What's wrong with me*, I silently wondered. *Don't panic.* I was hearing voices. *Hurry home. Move.* I experienced more rapid head throbbing and heart pounding. Now my palms were sweaty. Suddenly I found myself in front of Rosie's. *How did I get here so quickly?* I heard a male singer's voice crooning, from the jukebox, through the door. Suddenly I felt alarmed, too warm, even though it was my favorite time of year, October. Leaves of gold, yellow and reddish brown piled in small heaps in the gutters, co-mingled along the sidewalk vying for room underfoot.

Someone shouted, "Hey, Eleanor. I have a seat for you." I stared back looking dazed. My friend asked, "Where you going? You okay?"

"I have to get home right away. Something is happening." I tried to stay composed as I dashed away. I ran one block, two blocks, three blocks, hearing the crushing leaves beneath my feet. Four blocks. My heart was pounding fast. I couldn't stop running. Five blocks. Six blocks. Finally I reached Fairfax Street. Up three short steps to 1043 Eureka Flats, this place we called home. Just mother and me.

I flung open the door. Aunt Sally was standing behind mother, who was lying on the couch, a faint smile on her drawn face.

"You're here," mother whispered.

I backed out the door.

"Wait, mother," I said, half hushed, half shouting. "I'll get the doctor."

Again I felt compelled to run. Thank goodness for my track training. Again I counted blocks. I had no feeling of exhaustion. Two blocks to the doctor's office. I pushed open the door.

"It's mother," I gasped heavily.

"Eleanor," Dr. Levine looked up. "What's going on with your mother?"

"She doesn't look too good. She hasn't been eating and I'm really scared. Can you please come right away?"

"Let's go." Dr. Levine jumped up, snatched his black bag. We both ran to his car. He covered the two blocks in less than sixty seconds. I opened the door immediately, my eyes riveting toward the couch where mother was lying.

But we were too late. Aunt Sally glanced at us without a sound and pulled the cover over mother's head. I was dumbfounded.

Death news travels fast. Suddenly the whole neighborhood knew mother was gone. Earl's brother, Samuel, came immediately to our house straight from school, having heard I had left school upset. Neighbors brought plates of food, recalled stories about when my mother did something with them. They would not let Lois Mae, my younger brother or I lift a finger. My three older brothers were in the Army and Navy. They could not come home due to the severity of the war. The white families came in long cars, bringing flowers and baskets of food. They seemed pleased to meet Ophelia's children. The most astonishing gesture happened when the longest car I had ever seen parked out front. A chauffeur got out and knocked on our door.

"Does Mrs. Williams' family live here?" he inquired.

"Yes." I answered. He handed me a white envelope with a note signed Mrs. Rosa Abernathy, Earl's older sister. According to the note, she was providing us with a limousine service as long as we needed it. I was most grateful. "Thank you so much," I said. I was overcome with warmth and surprised by the outpouring of love. I had never imagined my mother knew so many people. Hundreds of people appeared at our small house during the entire weekend, right up to the burial date. Mother's passing overwhelmed us with sadness. She was only forty-five years old. Why now? Oh! Why now? Yes, Danielle there was sorrow in our lives. But the many joyful days I spent with mother will always be cherished.

Love,
Mama Curry

P.S. Here's an ironic thing about life. Sometimes it makes no sense at all. I had managed to save $423 dollars before mother's passing. I have my second chance to think about going to college. When mother died I had to use the money to bury her. She didn't have insurance. Another college opportunity was gone!

CHAPTER 6

▼

"WHAT WAS IT LIKE FALLING IN LOVE?"

Dear Danielle,

When your grandfather was courting me, he teasingly said, "Hey, Eleanor, let's get married and have a house full of children."

"Okay, I laughed. "How big will our house be? Why would we have so many children?"

"That's part of God's mystery," Papa Curry said, turning serious. "It's part of God's plan."

With mother gone, I didn't know what I was going to do. I remembered her telling me, "No matter what happens in life, keep the routine going." This meant school, yet I dreaded being alone. Papa Curry sent me a letter stating his decision to come home for Christmas and discuss plans to get married. He wanted to marry me! I read the letter for the next two months nearly every day. Me? Why had he chosen me? He could have the most beautiful girl or the richest in at least two states, yet he chooses me. Most of my life I had been around women, my mother, a sister, aunts, the teachers at school. The few teenage boys and uncles I knew were seldom in my view of the future. Well, that was before I met your grandfather. Marriage! I was skeptical about this gigantic move, though he persisted. I was a teen orphan, living alone. I was lacking knowledge about sex. The subject had never been discussed with me. However, I had heard during gym classes, from older girls, if one ever missed a monthly menstrual period, one might be pregnant.

We were two teenagers yearning for each other. I graduated from high school. He was still at Kentucky State College. October, November and early December dragged along. When he returned home and actually said to me, "Let's get married, I love you," I surrendered to him completely. I was eighteen and Papa Curry was twenty when we married His parents had to sign the marriage certificate before we could get married.

We were married in the spacious living room of Earl's mother's house on March 22, 1946. Rev. Mitchell read our marriage vows to us. He stated how, "...a man shall leave his father and mother and be joined unto his wife, and they shall be one flesh, and cling together for better or worse 'til death do them part, forsaking all others as long as they both shall live." (KJV).

That was another of God's great mysteries, I thought, as I had never heard such a dramatic utterance. Rev. Mitchell then told us to love one another as God loves us, and declared us married. After he pronounced us husband and wife, Papa Curry took both my hands in only one of his hands, kissed me and said, "The two of us are now one." This was the first time I focused on the size of his hands. Imagine one hand holding both of mine, a hand that was strong, steady and six-and-a-half inches wide, with a firm grip that took my breath away. When Papa Curry shakes someone's hand for the first time, they know their hand has been shook. When he held my hands, I felt like he was holding me.

We moved into the home of Cousin Emma on Papa Curry's side of the family. She had an extra bedroom and did not want to live by herself. We stayed with her for a few months until Papa Curry found a place for us to live.

I was captivated by your grandfather's romantic spirit. As well, I found him to be handsome, considerate, and a lot of fun. Plus, he appeared to have a deep sense of right from wrong. He was born in a generation when husbands were called "Head of Household," "Bread-winners" and "Protectors of the Family."

We were blissfully happy, exceptionally healthy and blindly in love, yet I was totally unprepared for the adjustment to married life. While courting, some of our habits and hobbies remained invisible. After we were married, I realized how little we really knew about each other. For example, I liked to dance, read, sing, drink Pepsi Cola and go out with close girl friends. Papa Curry liked to smoke, drink beer, play cards with his brothers late some nights and go to the racetrack. Was going out with girlfriends still happening? Not any more. Was playing cards late some nights still happening? Not any more.

What was the role of a husband and a wife once we were married? When I first got married I thought a wife was supposed to handle the necessities of the house and raise any children the couple had. I thought a husband was supposed to protect the family, love his wife and work. The minute our first daughter was born, I was abruptly thrust into another adjustment of married life. A baby. I knew nothing about babies. I don't remember ever being around anyone that small until I had our first child. Papa Curry had taken care of his younger brothers. He knew more about babies than I did.

Let me give you an example of Papa Curry's gentleness. I remember when Brenda was a few weeks old. She would cry. I would cry too, thinking she was hurt or something was wrong with her. Papa Curry would console me and pick Brenda up, simply saying to me, "Babies cry." He would rock her to sleep, usually going to sleep himself.

We were very close to each other, spending much time together. When Papa Curry would come home from work, after dinner he'd teach me how to play card games. My favorite was Honeymoon Whist, when only two people played. Next came Zero, when three people played. Finally, I graduated to Whist and Bid Whist, when four people played. Other evenings we'd play Scrabble, the word game. Just when I figured out how to beat him, Papa Curry would spell a seven-letter word and win the game.

Love
Mama Curry

CHAPTER 7

▼

"HOW DID YOU SURVIVE EIGHT KIDS?"

Danielle, Danielle, Danielle,

I really want to thank you for this amazing question: "How did I survive eight kids?" Up until now I seldom ever thought about it. I am overwhelmed even now, while attempting to glance back and reflect upon how a goodly portion of my life was spent. You bring tears to my eyes, being so sensitive. Just recognizing a woman needs much support raising one child, let alone eight, is a jolting experience. It happened so fast for me. Did I have time to think about it? Not until you called my attention to the whole notion. Honey, I really appreciate you bringing up the subject.

Once we were married and had children, our lives were completely changed. Let's look at the life of the babies from birth to three years old. The girls were born first, thirteen months apart. We named them Brenda, Bonnie and Barbara. Papa Curry had wanted boys. All the girls' names started with the letter "B." Next we had five boys, about two years apart. Their names are Richmond, Jr., and James, William (Bill) your Dad, Paul and David. Thank God the children came one at a time. They were all born completely healthy.

Generally speaking, I discovered each baby was very different. Yet we did the same basic things. It seemed natural, for example, to nurse our babies. I breast-fed the first five babies. However, I could only breast-feed the girls for five months before weaning due to another pregnancy. Our babies always slept in their own cribs. Once I had finished nursing them, I'd put them back in their cribs.

We anticipated behavior, setting up regular feeding times, sleeping times and playing times. I learned to sleep when they slept and get up when they awakened. They were healthy babies, none too fat or too thin. Of course, we took all of our babies in for regular check-ups, making sure they received all the necessary health shots. It was important for us to be good parents.

Danielle, to this day we often tell this story about Papa Curry: At his insistence, anyone who came to visit his first four babies had to wear masks (so as not to breathe on them) and stand back three feet. But with the last four, he didn't care who held them, fed them or played with them.

Another important point about parenting concerned me. As their mother, I seldom thought about my own needs, thinking mainly about our children's needs. Even before I was pregnant, I never smoked cigarettes or drank alcohol. I maintained healthy eating habits and had regular check-ups at the clinic. I always projected a pleasant disposition. This might not seem important to you now; however, one day it will make sense. We simply enjoyed being with each child. We were the parents, but at the same time, we learned so much from watching them grow. But most important, we wanted our home to be a place of love and affection. We wanted to protect and guard them from harm and danger. It was our duty and responsibility to demonstrate our love. We went through the terrible twos, the uncertain adolescents and the troublesome teens. Every phase was different for each one.

Danielle, I want to add one more story, here:

One day in 1994, I met Dr. Benjamin Spock, the renowned baby doctor. I was one of several panelists at a symposium for parents. The night before the event, the panelists were given fifteen minutes to talk with him one-on-one. Here is how our conversation went:

"Dr. Spock, it is good to meet you," I said. "I purchased a copy of the first book you printed in 1946 when my daughter was born."

"Do you still have a copy?" Dr. Spock asked.

"Oh, my goodness, no," I responded. "That was over forty-five years ago."

"Did you have any more children?" he asked.

"Yes," I said quickly, thinking about the fifteen-minute time limit. "We have three daughters and five sons."

"Are you serious?" He looked surprised. "How did you bring them up? What are they like? What did you do with them? Was it hard? Do you know what I mean?"

"Well," I was laughing after Dr. Spock's barrage of questions. "Our time is running out so I'll give you the short answers," I began. "We fed them three meals a day. We taught them to love each other and to respect other people. We made them obey their teachers. My husband would tell all of them, 'We will keep you home until you turn eighteen years old, go to college, join the service, have a job, or get married.' None of our children ever ran away from home. Some might have thought it, yet it never happened."

"My land, Eleanor," Dr. Spock said, astonished. "You should be writing books and telling people exactly what you just told me."

"Dr. Spock," I said, laughing again. "My fifteen minutes are up. Don't parents already know this stuff?"

"No, Eleanor," he replied. "Some people don't even realize babies have to eat one meal a day, let alone three. Some parents demand their kids get out of the house before they become teenagers. So get busy and write that book."

So, after that, Danielle, I was ready and started writing.

I love you,
Mama Curry

CHAPTER 8

▼

"HOW DID YOU STAY SANE RAISING EIGHT CHILDREN?"

Dear Danielle,

I bore eight children over a span fourteen years. It took thirty-two years to raise them all. Papa Curry and I did it together. We had much help from Papa Curry's mother, sisters and brothers, neighbors and friends, principals and teachers. So, Danielle, another question might be, "Why did we have so many kids?"

I asked myself that question after the girls were born. Some of my friends were upset because they could not get pregnant, while the doctor told me I was very healthy and fertile. Once this was clear, my other reason had to be the noticeable differences in each baby. All of our daughters were beautiful babies and all of our sons were handsome babies. I was also fascinated at how they all resembled us, yet were uniquely themselves. Here is an example of how each child reacted very differently to the same situation—starting kindergarten.

(1951) Brenda decided I should stay with her, and it took three weeks to make her stay.

(1952) Bonnie was ready and wanted me to go back home.

(1953) Barbara did not want to go. She decided to go because her sisters were there.

(1956) Richmond conquered the backyard at five years old. "Stay close to the house so you won't get lost," I warned. "Momma, I know," he replied. "I go to school and don't get lost."

(1958) Arnold was ready to, "Be with the little people so I can play with them."

(1961) Bill would have rather been at home. He thought the teacher smelled funny. He said she drank beer.

(1963) Paul was full of smiles, ready to go, "Because we all go to school."

(1965) David wanted to know, "What's school for anyway?"

Due to their age differences, all eight children were rarely home at the same time of day. Since they were spread apart over a fourteen-year span, at one point we were parenting three teenage girls, four mid-size boys and one baby boy. Each age group needed a different type of attention.

Counting parents, there were ten of us living in our home in San Francisco from 1960 to 1964. During that time, Papa Curry was working two jobs. He was a construction laborer from seven-thirty in the morning to four-thirty in the afternoon, Monday through Friday. He would come home, take a shower, eat dinner and go back out to the second job cleaning doctors' offices in a large building in San Mateo from seven to nine in the evening.

Meanwhile, I was busy taking care of our home, a real big job, which covered shopping, preparing three meals each day and delegating age appropriate tasks for each child old enough to assume household chores. I mainly guided the children in emotional areas and covered homework, social activities and community affairs.

Danielle, I must also tell you about why we came to California. How did we decide to move to San Francisco? Papa Curry often told stories to your aunts and uncles about having the faith of a "mustard seed." (Your dad was not born yet.)

In spite of working two jobs while living in St. Louis, we seldom had enough money to last until the next paycheck. Papa Curry would come home tired and weary, yet one particular night there was a glimmer of excitement in his words.

"Sweetheart, I have come to a major decision," he began. We're moving to California. I'll go first, get a job, and then send for you and the kids." He paused, and rushed on. "I'm working two jobs, taking care of you and our five kids. We pay rent and barely cover our food bill. Forget about recreation. I'm sick of it. It's time to make a move. Are you with me?"

I stood there speechless. I thought to myself, 'you *have lost it*'. I opened my mouth but no words would come out.

"Come on, come on, talk," Papa Curry said anxiously. "What do you think?"

"You're in charge." I stammered. "Why are you asking me?"

"Good," Papa Curry smiled. "That means yes."

"When are you leaving?" I whispered.

"Next week!" Papa Curry stated with manly conviction. Before I could think about how our lives were about to change, Papa Curry had packed our station wagon and left town.

The news and the leaving shocked me. Three days and two nights later, Papa Curry called me from California.

"Eleanor! I'm in San Mateo, California. I need your help. I forgot my sister's telephone number."

"What sister?" I was still numb over the fact that he had left.

"Think, Eleanor. It has to be Alice, the one in California. Right?"

Six months later, Papa Curry sent four train tickets. He called to make sure the tickets had arrived and inquired about when we planned to leave. After realizing we needed six tickets, Papa Curry laughed, explaining how he had forgotten he had five children. It was hard to find a house large enough for us to rent, so he mentioned less kids. One week later he sent two more tickets. Papa Curry had kept his promise. We were headed on a train to California.

Four days later we arrived in San Francisco, California. He had found a small house in the Ocean-view housing Project District. My first glimpse of the area shocked me. The house was hidden from the main street. Trees ten feet plus, stood in a city block long close together, but not touching. Aunt Adele's (Poppa Curry's sister) car made a right turn onto a semi-dirt road. I stared in disbelief. Rows of small houses were built on stilts on dirt spaces. No grass, no sidewalks, no street lights. It was midday with no people in sight either. Aunt Adele told me "I hope you like it. This was the best he could do for now." I swallowed trying to conceal my disappointment. There was some privacy. We squeezed the two of us and five children into three bedrooms, a large kitchen, one bathroom and no living room.

The workings inside the household were complex, with many activities happening daily. Every single week, Sunday through Saturday, certain things had to be done to maintain order and keep operations smooth. This included such things as packing lunches, taking care of anything that popped up and getting bus cards for transportation to school. We all rode the city buses, except for Papa Curry. He had traded in the station wagon for a blue pick-up truck, which he drove back and forth to the construction site and back and forth to the cleaning job. We found a larger place and moved to the Hunter's Point Housing Projects in 1958.

Our days became busier, following a regime that went something like this:

Sunday's routine: Once we became members of Bayview Lutheran Church in 1960, we remembered the Sabbath, 'to keep it holy.' This meant Sunday school and church services. A funny thing often happened as we prepared for church. One of the younger boys would always misplace a sock. If the sock couldn't be found by 10:30 a.m., one of the teenage girls would have to stay home with her younger brother.

Sunday dinner was especially important. This was the day for plenty of fried chicken (two chickens cut up into about twenty-one pieces), home made potato salad and canned peas. Jell-O with fruit cocktail was the favorite dessert.

Monday's routine: Change five beds, wash six to eight bunches of clothes, hang clothes on clotheslines (did not a have clothes dryer) and prepare dinner. Weekday dinners were very important for two reasons: Papa Curry was always ready to eat after a hard day at work, and dinner was the only time we could all be together to share the day's happenings. On Mondays we had ham hocks with great northern beans, tossed salad, cornbread and a sheet of apple cobbler, which guaranteed the beans would be eaten.

Tuesday's routine: Fold all the clothes. Iron those that needed it and put them away in their exact places. Teach girls how to sew. Homemade biscuits with syrup, smothered cabbage—sprinkled with crumbled bacon—and creamed style canned corn was Tuesday's dinner. This was our meatless day, due to the heavy meal the day before.

Wednesday's routine: Shampoo, dry, press and comb the girls' hair in various styles. (I had to learn how to do this, as I had never done hair before.) The girls had their hair combed and braided every morning before leaving for school. Mustard, turnip and collard greens with ham hocks, baked sweet potatoes and homemade cornbread were on the menu for Wednesdays.

Thursday's routine: Clean bathrooms. Pick up the house and keep an assemblage of order. Wash clothes, as Thursday was considered mid-week. Leftovers became "Mama's Specialty" for dinner. This could be anything, with a few shrimps thrown in. Ketchup was the main thing though; it camouflaged the leftovers and tricked the mind into believing the meal was fresh-made. "We better eat the food first time it's cooked," one daughter said, "while we know what it is."

Friday's routine: Friday was payday. I was never unhappy on payday. Even if the money ran out before the next paycheck, I stayed happy. Nobody wants to give up "hard earned money" to a sad, mad face. So I was always glad on payday. Friday's dinner was usually spaghetti, coleslaw, fried Jack salmon and toasted French bread.

Saturday's routine: Clean up the living room. Take the boys to the barber (one Saturday a month) hot dogs and pork-and-beans with Kool-Aid for dinner. Snack food was unheard of during those times, so we drank Kool-Aid, which was a real treat to all of us.

Then there were the special days, the holidays. Danielle, we enjoyed the major holidays every year, especially loving certain foods, which were significant to each holiday.

New Year's Day: Chitterlings, black-eyed peas, coleslaw, hot water cornbread and apple pie. Generations past would say, "Chitterlings at ten pounds for twenty-five cents kept us alive, and black-eyed peas brought us good luck all year long."

Valentine's Day: Cherry pie signifies love God, yourself and your neighbor.

St. Patrick's Day: Corned beef, cabbage, red potatoes and carrots.

Easter: After attending church, renewing the fact that 'Christ is risen' we were thankful for God's bountiful gifts. On Easter we had baked ham, greens, potato salad, and lemon pie.

Mother's Day: Papa Curry would cook breakfast. I would get cards galore, often hand made by the kids.

Memorial Day: Bar-B-Q ribs, baked beans, carrot and celery sticks, Pepsi Cola.

Father's Day: We cooked breakfast for Papa Curry. He would get cards galore.

Independence Day: Fourth of July picnic at the park, baskets full of food and watermelon.

Labor Day: We just rested.

Thanksgiving Day: This was always an awesome, serious celebration in our home. I discovered from my chef brother how to cook a turkey all night long. I would take an evening nap about six o'clock the night before, then wake up at eight-thirty to start cooking. At midnight I'd place the turkey in the oven at 300 degrees. The next morning the aroma would awaken the entire family, thankful and anticipating dinner. The menu was always traditional: turkey with cornbread stuffing, mashed potatoes, sweet peas, tossed salad, cranberry sauce and half a dozen sweet potato pies. We recited what we were thankful for. We blessed the food, especially the day. We relaxed after dinner, too full to move.

Christmas Day: Papa Curry has always been absolutely the best Christmas tree decorator. When he finished our tree every year, everyone marveled at its beauty. First, he insisted on the tree being freshly cut. It had to be at least five to six feet high. Then he'd plan a color scheme. Next he would unpack the decorations from the closets, and then he would start stringing lights around the tree. Papa Curry insisted that the tree always have plenty of lights. When Xavier, one of our great-grandchildren, was twelve years old, he was awestruck by beauty of our tree.

"Papa Curry's Christmas tree gets your whole attention," he exclaimed to his grandmother one year.

Once all of our children had moved to far-flung cities with their own families, we still came together to celebrate Christmas Eve at our home. Rarely if ever have all of them been able to come every year, but those who were still in the area managed to come to our house. We celebrated the birth of Jesus Christ, reading from our family bible. We sang carols, and had anyone less than twelve years old perform or share things they had learned in school. We exchanged gifts, either made or bought. We took pictures to share later. I cooked from scratch, serving two large pots of chili. Everyone brought a favorite dish. I also prepared twelve sweet potato and mince-apple pies. The pies were gifts for each family to take home.

Birthdays: Whenever it was someone's birthday, I served that child's favorite cake and ice cream.

Danielle, on the rest of the days of the year, I always had to awaken everybody to make sure they were not late for school. It seemed as though I was constantly coaxing, "Get up, come and eat breakfast. Hurry up, children." Often, no one responded to my first calling. One school day, Papa Curry was off from work. "Honey," I said to

Papa Curry in desperation. "How did your mother ever get you and your six brothers out of bed to come eat breakfast before you guys went to school?"

"She certainly didn't use cold cereal," he smiled. "Mama got up at five-thirty in the morning. We would smell bacon, scrambled eggs, hot biscuits and hot cocoa. Feet would start hitting the floor, sailing to the bathroom, washing up and flying down the steps before all the food disappeared."

By the 1960s, we had, as I mentioned earlier, become members of Bayview Lutheran Church in San Francisco. A whole new world opened up for me: Volunteerism! I became President of the Lutheran Faith Ladies Guild, President of the Bret Harte PTA, and Chairwoman of the Bayview District Council/United Community Fund, all in a span of two years. How did we keep all these things straight? We did so by realizing it was better to live one day at a time.

But can you imagine David, the youngest child in our extremely busy household, trying to figure his family out? When David was about four years old, I began working on Saturdays to help out with money. One evening David had his toys scattered over the living room. Here's what happened:

"David," I say calmly, "Pick your toys up."

"Shut up and tend to your own business," He replied defiantly.

"Come here," I said, shocked by his attitude.

David ran out of the room and hid in the closet.

"Something's wrong with David," one brother whispered. "He told Mama to shut up."

Baffled, I decided to take him to the pediatrician a couple days later. When we arrived, I explained to the doctor what had happened. He asked if David's father disciplined him and if this ever happened with his dad.

"No," I replied. "It has never happened with any of our other children either."

The doctor turned to David.

"Come over here, David," he said calmly. David did not move.

"Come here right now." The doctor stated firmly. David started to cry and moved toward the doctor.

"Good, David," the doctor reassured him. "I want to ask you a few questions, and your mommy will be here with us. What's your mommy's name?"

"Brenda, Bonnie, Barbara and Eleanor," David said without hesitation.

"Who are these people?" The doctor turned to me whispering and looking perplexed.

"Oh, those are his three big sisters and I'm Eleanor," I said.

"David," the doctor was patient. "Tell me about your mommy named Brenda."

"She likes me," David replied. "We play and she reads me stories."

"What about the one named Bonnie?"

"Bonnie makes me take a nap, tells me to stop being messy and be quiet."

"What about the one named Barbara?"

"Barbara makes me laugh. We go to the park to play."

"Tell me about the one named Eleanor."

"She's the girl mommy and she's gone all the time."

The doctor laughed and then got serious.

"David has what is called role confusion. Since all of you are about the same size, he doesn't know who the mother is. You'll have to have the girls stop telling him what to do. You handle the discipline for the next six months. Call me back if you need me." I learned a valuable lesson about listening to the youngest child's thoughts.

See you later, Danielle,
Mama Curry

CHAPTER 9

▼

"WHY IS FAMILY IMPORTANT TO YOU?

Do you believe in hitting children?
How do you cope with being down or angry?
Does anything scare you?"

Dear Danielle,

Our family tree has several branches, many of which are not detailed
in this writing due to the inherent enormity of such an undertaking.
However, I did receive some questions from two of your second cousins,
Nicole and Aja Perry. They live in Chicago, Illinois and are the grandchildren of Papa Curry's youngest brother, Michael Leonard Curry. Their
questions, (shown above) were different from yours, so I've included them
as well.

Why Family is Important to Me

Family is important because it is God's plan to provide a safe place
for people to dwell, take care of each other and love each other. God
tells us to be fruitful and multiply the earth. One of the best

oft-repeated remarks is, "Be it ever so humble, there is no place like home." Home is where you should be able to be yourself and get any type of support you need. Our family stayed together, prayed most of the time together and played together. We spent weekends at various parks, most notably Central Park in San Mateo. We all played card games, Scrabble and worked puzzles. Papa Curry and I took our kids to most everything that was free. We enrolled then in Camp Fire Girls at the appropriate age. They did chores, which were evenly divided among the older children. I taught the boys how to cook, sew and take care of themselves. If they ever married they would appreciate their wives more. I taught the girls the same so they could take care of their families.

Family also means taking care of children when they are sick. I remember when the girls were five, four and three years old. They all caught chickenpox. They were ill from Thanksgiving until Christmas Even that year. I was bone tired. Luckily, we seldom had any more complicated illness than that one. Our standard treatment for minor colds was chicken soup, hot tea and bed rest all day. There was not any TV at that time, only radio. Bed rest was real rest.

My Feelings about Hitting Children

No! I definitely do not believe in hitting children. I was never hit as a child, so I followed similar rules taught to me. The old biblical adage, "Spare the rod and spoil the child" does not mean hit the child. It means guide, lead and protect the child from dangerous encounters. A rod and a staff are made to comfort, not hit. Most children who are beaten by parents or other adults probably end up doing the same thing to others when they are big enough.

Still, I remember realizing my style of bringing up children was different from Papa Curry's. He was brought up in a strict home where hitting children was considered the proper form of discipline. My upbringing, as you've seen in these pages, was quite different. My mother took a more lenient approach, employing guidance and natural consequences as a way for us to learn. Papa Curry and I had several discussions about child rearing. Since I was home the most, my style prevailed. One major thing was obvious about Papa Curry that I loved. His voice made the kids do exactly as they were told immediately. I call it the "male voice." If, for example, I told any of them to do something they would rather not do, they might then go ask their dad in an attempt to get a "yes" answer.

"What did your mother say?" Papa Curry would calmly ask. "That's what you will do." End of the conversation. So I don't believe you should ever hit a child for his or her own good. Before Papa Curry and I discovered that hitting children would cause damage to them, some of our children were spanked when they were younger. I prayed for that form of discipline to stop, especially once they became teenagers. We simply found new methods. Once knowing better, we did better.

Coping with that "Down" Feeling

I actually remember one specific 'down' time for me. After Mother died, my best friend's mother died the following week. I went to her mother's funeral to give moral support. The minute I glanced at the coffin, I saw a reflection of my own mother's face. I could not stop crying. I remained on my knees, tears flowing unstoppable. I was grief stricken. But someone lifted me gently up and let me cry. I felt fine once it was released.

Down moments make me want to be alone. I cry. I go see a funny movie. I have faith that I'll get over the situation. I seldom talk to anybody when I'm experiencing bad times. I'm too disgusted, embarrassed or upset. I pray. I ask God to help me rise above the circumstance of the moment. I pray before I go to sleep. I awaken ready for a new day. Even if I do such things, though, sometimes a down feeling can linger. So I repeat my actions. Then I sing a song.

Danielle, I'm fondly attached to a relationship with two women who entered my life in 1967. It would be impossible to answer the question about ways to feel better and not tell you about these two friends who are closer to me than natural-born sisters. Just like me, they each have a husband. They both have worked at the San Mateo Unified School District where we met. What are their names? What are the main characteristics that bind us together? How do the three of us care about other people? What makes people think we're courageous? Why does it take nerve to tell the truth? Due to our individual uniqueness, we each have a particular style emphasizing our methods of handling differences. The story of our friendship has grown stronger and better every year.

Papa Curry first told me about Claire Mack after doing being hired by Eddy, her husband to add family room to their home. Claire and Eddy owned their home in San Mateo.

"Hey, Eleanor, I met a woman today who acts just like you," Papa Curry said. "She's always doing things in the community too. I think you'll find her interesting."

A few months after meeting Claire, we bought a house and moved to San Mateo. Six months later I was hired by the San Mateo Elementary School District. The District was at the height of implementing a new desegregation school plan, to insure equality of education within all its schools. Claire was hired because of her love of children. She approached a friend of hers who was employed by Pacific Telephone Company. "I have a great new stimulating job for you," Claire told her friend, demanding she, "Quit that job you have and come work with our kids. They need you." The following week Claire introduced me to Erma Jean Prothro.

Danielle, you might ask 'what unique characteristics did these two women have causing the growth of the friendship'? When I first met Claire and Erma it became obvious we might easily work together, due to a strong sense of self. Claire cares by using direct confrontational conversation, like it or not. She steadfastly believes in telling the truth as she sees it. "I have something to tell you that you need to know," Claire will begin. "I ought not to tell you, but I'm telling you anyway. It's for your own good." Then she'll tell you exactly what she thinks you need to know. When life seems too hard and no one stands ready to make a decision, Claire enters, assesses the situation, makes a decision and takes action. Her no-nonsense approach to life has earned her the nickname Mack-Attack.

Now, Erma cares by listening intently, asking questions until you get the point. She believes in the advantage of prayer. Her method of admonishment is asking the right questions. For example, Erma might ask, "Why do you want to do that?" or "I don't really believe you want to do that," or "Are you crazy? You're just kidding, right?" Whether moments are too relaxed or extremely tense, Erma can give a kindly laugh that gets everybody back on track. Erma is affectionately known by a multitude of nephews and nieces as Aunt Babe.

My way of caring is by searching for different points of view, seeking facts and seeing many sides to the same problem. My best strength and favorite technique is guessing. For example, I'll say to myself, *'That didn't work. I guess I'll try something else'*. I discovered early in life the power of praying, though I did not know at that time what I was doing. I was afraid of God until I realized God represents love, not hate. Now I have nothing to fear because faith wipes out fear.

Later in life, I studied and found God's goodness and abundant love. I now know the power of prayer and practice praying daily. Praying is a powerful action where we listen and talk with God. God is love, and showers us with love so we can give love to others. In fact, Danielle, your name for me, and a name my closest friends use too, the endearing name, "Mama Curry," reminds me of the motherly love I am able to share because of God and prayer I'm able to share because of courage. We three, Claire, Erma, and I, have been friends for nearly forty years. People who know us well call each of us courageous.

Throughout the turbulent 1970s and 1980s, we have encountered many emotional challenges. When speaking during the Civil Rights Movement and desegregation of the various school districts in California, we often had to stand firm in defense of our rights as Americans. We had to stand and defend the educational needs of African American children. We did not support 'special ed' for little black boys. Those were often controversial times. After one heated incident at a conference in Monterey, for example, courageous was not the word the opposition used to describe us. Instead they called us "cocky broads." Just for the record, "broad" means, *large in extent from one side to the other, extensive, wide-ranging, full and clear,* and *explicit.* While this description definitely fit us, we certainly were not the kind of "broads" they had in mind.

We have handled dissension, oppression, racism and sexism. Claire, especially, has faced seemingly impossible situations that needed correcting. Every single time she has placed herself squarely in the middle of various issues. She doesn't back down. She works through it. Facing similar obstacles, Erma remains humble. She is bold and persistent, dedicating her life to strengthening families regardless of their race, creed or status in life. I, on the other hand, have preferred to give out helpful information about my own experiences, particularly in the areas of marriage, child rearing, health, women or money matters.

The three of us chose to give help, support and love wherever needed. We have shared our knowledge, laughter and sadness, but mostly our joy. We've had fun times. Mainly our hearts have always been open for each other. To tell the truth always takes nerve. It takes love too. Do you know the glue that really bonds us together? The glue is our love for the Lord.

Claire, her husband Eddie, their three grown daughters and two grandchildren has certainly made an impact in the City of San Mateo. Erma, her husband John, one grown daughter, two grown sons and six grandchildren personifies the Christian spirit visible in their lives. Earl and I, three grown daughters, five grown sons, twenty-three grandchildren and sixteen great-grandchildren represent our thoughts of caring, sharing and fair play. We have 180 years of experiences within the three families. We thank God for the fellowship. We are blessed with almost forty years of best friendship and sisterhood. If you can count five friends on one hand, count yourself blessed.

Another extremely close friend I met in the 1970s at Menlo Atherton High School was Viola White. 'Vi,' a vivacious, infectious woman has been a consultant in the field of human relations in San Mateo County. Most importantly, Vi is a walking encyclopedia regarding God, the Bible and all its ramifications. After a few conversations, for example, and under her guidance, I began telling whoever would listen that she was my Spiritual Advisor. Vi always places God first. She has a spiritual focus on every issue under discussion.

One time, William C., a young man who had just received his Doctorate of Psychology from Stanford University, requested a lunch with Vi and me. Listen to the start of our conversation.

"Life seems rather complicated," Dr. C. said. "Even with my recent degree, I ponder the purpose of life and where one starts."

"Well you always start with God, as far as I'm concerned," Vi responded. "You see, God hates wickedness, but not with a wicked hate."

"I never found that in any of my studies," Dr. C. said, inquisitively. "Where did you learn such a thing?" This one comment turned into a captivating afternoon.

The more Vi and I worked together, the more respect we held for each other. On a few occasions I heard her speak in public forums. During one of the those engagements I was so impressed with her message from God and how she inspired the audience that I wrote down many of her words from that evening. I sent these words to her as a birthday gift of expressions entitled *Spiritual Explosives* by Viola White. She was jubilant.

Several months later Vi surprised me by submitting my name to an award committee in conjunction with the *San Francisco Foundation*. The theme for Vi's essay about me was based on a quote from Emerson: "Great hearts send forth steadily the secret forces that incessantly draw great events." Vi further wrote, "Who are the great hearts? They are those people who dare to think and radiate great thoughts and great expectancies of success, prosperity, and good instead of failure, trouble and limitations." Yes, she was referring to me as one of those "great hearts." Guess what happened? Two weeks later a representative from the selection committee called Vi's house to announce the winner. As fate would have it, I was sitting at her dining room table. She answered the telephone and said, "She's right here. Thank you, thank you, and thank you." Vi hung up the phone and said to me, "Girl, I sent your name to the *San Francisco Foundation* for an award and you won." Needless to say, I was flabbergasted.

Later I discovered details about Vi's life. She's been married to Dr. Andrew W. White for forty-eight years. They met at Houston College for Negroes. They moved to Washington, D. C. to attend Howard University. They graduated in 1949 and married that same year. They have three daughters: Marlys, a teacher; Tamera, a crime prevention trainer; and Vaneida, a family practice physician. Dr. White has touched hundreds of lives through his service to the community. Excellence in medical care has been his hallmark. For more than forty years, the Peninsula Community has benefited from house calls that were a key to his success. His friendly, warm and easy-going bedside manner has endeared him to thousands of Bay Area patients and hospital staff. Many citizens paid tribute to Dr. White in 1998, affirming how he and Vi are another pair of "great hearts." It is great hearts like these that give me reprieve from feeling down by giving me reason to feel love and hope.

Dealing with Anger

Sometimes I have experienced deep anger. When President John Kennedy was assassinated, I was shocked, speechless, extremely sad and numb for several days. When the first news of Dr. Martin Luther King's assassination came, I experienced bouts of additional shock, utter disbelief and intolerable anger. I wondered what in the world was wrong. I thought, why *are they killing our leaders? What is this?* I shamelessly cried out loud and remember my telephone ringing.

"Hello," I mumbled, fighting back my tears.

"What's wrong?" the speaker inquired. "Sounds like you're crying."

"They shot Dr. King," I said, still weeping.
"Oh! I'm so sorry," the speaker said, "I didn't know you cried."
"Who is this?" I asked, amazed at my calmness. Now the caller was crying too.
"What can we do?" she questioned. "Please stop crying. What can we do? Oh God!"

Calls poured into our home for the next week, day and night. In many parts of the country where African American people lived, fires were set. This was the result of a deep sense of frustration many citizens felt. We advised those who called to light a candle and pray for Dr. King's family. Anger became peace, appropriate to Dr. King's non-violence stand.

But today we don't have to suffer feeling down or cope with being angry. We don't have to be depressed or "have the blues." There are plenty of people who are here to help. One of the best sources of advice during the first fifteen years of our marriage came from relatives and a few trusted close neighbors. After 1960, though, I turned to ministers, therapy sessions plus any self-help group that related to my specific issues. I have not had to use these services frequently. However, I am grateful they now exist.

Dealing with Fear

One thing that really scared me happened in 1948 in St. Louis. We were forced to move into a condemned house. We had no idea what that meant. Papa Curry worked nights. Our third baby was due any day. I was relaxed. It was early October. When I went to bed that night, I heard loud thumping noises in the dark. Thump, thump, scratching on the floor. *What in the world?* My heart was pounding louder than echoes of a drumbeat. I froze, too panicked to move. The light switch across the room right near the babies' cradle was unreachable. *My babies*, I thought, *my babies. Something is after my babies.* I dashed across the room and snatched on the light. Several gray field rats dashed away, blinded by the light, scurrying back behind the heavy cedar sliding doors. I started crying at the sight of them. I pulled the crib to the center of the room. I pulled at our bed, but it wouldn't move. I turned on every light in the house. I couldn't stop crying. The babies, one and two years old, did not even wake up. I jumped in the middle of our bed, wrapped my arms around myself and didn't move until dawn. Papa Curry came home around five that morning, rushing up the stairs two at a time. He had noticed the lights were all on. When he heard what had happened, he was very concerned. He found another place for us to live before the week came to an end. Danielle, Papa Curry is a very sensitive man and definitely one who protects his family. He helped me overcome obstacles and fight my fears.

Love you,
Mama Curry

CURRY FAMILY

Left to right: Barbara, age 12; Bonnie, age 13; Richmond Earl Curry, age 35; David, age 1; Eleanor Curry, age 33; Brenda, age 14; James Arnold, age 8; Paul, age 3; William (Bill), age 4; Richmond, Jr., age 9.

Mother's Day, May 1961
Bayview Lutheran Church
San Francisco, California

PART II

▼

How Our Children Saw It

CHAPTER 10

▼

Dear Danielle,

The following pages contain comments from your dad, aunts and uncles. Each tells what life was like for them living with Papa Curry and me.

Mama Curry

To Danielle from Aunt Brenda
Comedy Time, Dad and Mama

My father is the greatest man I have ever known. He is very religious, believing in God and the Ten Commandments.

During my early teen years, we lived in the Alice Griffins Public Housing Projects near Candlestick Park in San Francisco. My father was not only a carpenter; he was a very determined man. Seldom if ever has my father been offered a challenge from which he shied away. You know what he did when we moved into our new house in Alice Griffins? He called the Housing Authority and told them he didn't like the way the new house was built.

"Everything is running together from the living room straight to the dining room," he stated. "The kids won't know where to socialize or where to eat. I'd like to build a partition to separate the long room."

"Well, Mr. Curry," the voice on the phone said, "You can build a wall if you don't put any nails in the ceiling or the floor." Daddy was full of chuckles when telling us about the response he got. "Those people don't think you can put up a wall without any nails in the floor or ceiling, but I'm going to show them how to do it," he said.

Honey, my father put that wall up without any nails. This happened in 1964; forty years later, that wall is still standing. On top of that, everything he fixed was done with a hammer, nails and a pair of pliers. One day he was about to fix the television set.

"Mama, Daddy's getting ready to work on the TV with a hammer," I said, amazed. "You'd better come quickly. He's taking the nails out of his overalls right now!"

"Take cover," Mama laughed.

My father seldom if ever missed going to work. Well that is unless somebody mistreated any of us at school. Whenever that happened, Daddy would head for school in a suit, mind you. You see, it was unusual to see a black man walking around in a suit that often, especially in the projects. This was simply unheard of. So some of the kids from school started passing the word:

"Mr. Curry put on a suit today. Mr. Curry put on a suit." They actually followed Daddy to school. When he arrived and went into the office, the kids crowded around, looking through windows just to see what was going to transpire.

"Mr. Curry," some kids called out. "Mr. Curry is meeting the teacher." When my father shook the teacher's hand, one kid yelled out, "Uh oh! There goes another set of fingers." Another kid hollered, "Mr. Curry has a grip, man!"

Here's another thing about my father. His philosophy is, "Life is for the strong." To prove it, he actually pulls his own teeth—'with a pair pliers'. He even offered (jokingly) to pull ours too. "Your kids' teeth are not lumber," Mama would say.

But Danielle, I'm so glad your grandmother is my mother. Growing up with Mama was an exciting adventure. Besides taking dutiful care of us when we were growing up, she was then and has remained a really fun person. I'll never forget my first day of school. I had spent just over five years with my wonderful mother and two younger sisters. She made our clothes, read to us, rode us on her bike and sang us to sleep at night. We were never away from her. She took me to school that first day and told me, "Good-bye. I'll be back later."

Danielle, I had a fit. "Why are you leaving me?" I cried out. "Where are you going?" I grabbed her hand and would not let go. This went on for about a week. The tears did not work. Finally I gave up.

Before we moved to California, right across the street from where we lived stood a big church and day school. I was school age (around seven or eight) and noticed that all the white kids went to that school.

"Why can't we go to the school across the street with the white kids, Mama?" I asked.

"Because that's a Catholic school," Mama told me. She wanted to spare me the humiliation of the whole "whites only" nonsense.

When I decided to try my hand at stand-up comedy, one of the first venues I performed at was 'The Punch-line Comedy Club' in San Francisco.

Here's my opening comment:

"My mother knows a lot about love and nothing about sex."

"Are you the only kid?" A heckler shouted back.

"Nope, there are eight of us." Spontaneous laughter erupted.

"Your mom knows about sex, she just never told you."

I went home later to discuss sexual issues with Mama.

Danielle, Mama talked about loving your neighbor, be kind to little children and be good to your sisters and brothers.

"What about sex, Mama?" I ask perplexed.

"Oh," she looked at me. "You need to learn the difference between *loves*, *like* and *lust*. Your father likes candy, candles and carnations."

I was right, Danielle. Mama knows a lot about love and nothing about sex.

See you later,
Aunt Brenda

To Danielle from Aunt Bonnie

First off you should know I have never met anyone who speaks as well as my father. This includes teachers, actors, announces, politicians, doctors, lawyers and anybody else you've ever heard speak whose delivery inspired you. Your grandfather has a command of the English language, barring none, and a vocabulary that kept me running to the dictionary during my formative years. I put his eloquence in speaking right up there with Dr. Martin Luther King, Jr., and all the other great orators. As a matter of fact, one day Daddy came home and told us he had auditioned for, and won, the role of Dr. King in an upcoming movie. We were jumping up and down with excitement, giggling and telling him how proud we felt, when all of a sudden he said, "April fool!" Well of course we were dumbstruck because we knew that if they were going to make such a movie, he would be the perfect choice since he spoke so well. For a moment I didn't believe the *April fool* part. But it was pretty funny.

When I was in a creative writing class in college, we were asked to write a "portrait" about someone interesting. I chose my dad. Here is an excerpt from that essay.

Portrait of My Father

Family. Those people you live with. The ones you test and try things out on, and cry with and hopefully laugh with. Take my father, for example. Growing up with him wasn't always easy. I used to tell Mother that Daddy was only good at teaching me how not to raise my own children. I gave him the nickname "City Hall" because when he told us something, well, that was it. There was no changing his mind and you had better do as he said.

It didn't matter that all the other kids in the neighborhood got to do whatever they wanted, like attend community dances at the local gym or stay out late.

"Those kinds of things attract undesirables," was what he'd tell us. "You're not going." In short, no one was good enough for my father's children. If he had his way, none of us would ever have left home. You may think I'm making this up, but my father has emphatically made this very remark on a number of occasions: "If it were up to me, none of you would ever leave home. I'd build a tall fence around my house and my policy would be nobody in, nobody out." He'd say this with a tinge of laughter, but deep down I think he really meant it. What I didn't know at that time was that because of his love for us, he shuddered to even think of the dark roads we might cross during this journey called life. So, in his way of thinking, perhaps, better not to leave at all.

Yet leave the nest I did, laden with most of the character traits necessary to survive in the adult world, the ones you can only get from being part of a family. My most vivid childhood memory of my dad is the strength he exuded in all he did, including chastising his children.

His massive size (a towering six feet and 280 pounds.) and thundering voice were like the wrath of God coming to get us back in line. I say God instead of the devil because I knew then, as I do now, that he loved us. It's just that as a child, one doesn't feel that much love is needed. So profound was his presence that if I had indeed misbehaved, tears would come to my eyes before Daddy ever uttered a word. Talking back to Mom or Dad or lying was out of the question. We were much better off confessing if guilty and agreeing not let the transgression happen again. Mostly we'd get off with a thunderous lecture on character building, morality and the importance of obeying one's parents.

Of the entire thing kids get themselves into, it bothered my father most when we fought amongst ourselves. "You can pick your friends but God gives you your family," was how he'd put it. To him and years later to us, this meant no room for anything but love for this exclusive group.

Just as there were guidelines for our interactions with family members, guidelines also existed for interactions with the rest of the world. Respect was definitely in. This meant with teachers, shopkeepers, bus drivers, mailmen, neighbors or any other humans we encountered, especially if they were older than we were. Yes sir, no sir, yes ma'am and no ma'am are social graces that have remained with me over the years.

I still have crystal clear memories of my father shedding his carpenter's uniform in exchange for a dark suit, white shirt and tie for a trip to school to ascertain why I couldn't stop chewing gum in math class. It didn't matter that all the kids thought he was handsome and scurried to find out who he was. I sure wasn't going to claim him under the circumstances. I did, however, give up gum chewing in class.

Dad also came to school when the cafeteria workers refused to serve my younger sister lunch because she arrived at school too late for the morning lunch-count. He found this rationale absurd. Without profanity or raising his voice, he let the principal know just how he expected his children to be treated. Once the principal understood, that's how the school personnel treated us—with respect. After that day it never mattered what time they took the lunch count or if we were late. We were always served lunch.

From my father I learned how to stand my ground. Thanks to him, nobody ever pushes me around, and I always get what I want by respecting others and making sure others respect me.

During my early years in the 1950s, many households in our neighborhood had no fathers present. I thought this was strange and felt secure in the knowledge my father would never abandon us or even consider divorce, both for the love he held for our mother and all of his kids. He would tell us as much on many occasions. "I hope I'm never in a situation where I have to sacrifice one child to save another," he'd say. "I just don't think I could make such a decision. I love you guys so much that I don't ever want anything bad to happen to any of you. I know I couldn't choose one of you over the other." Now that's an awesome thing to contemplate when you're only a child. Believe me, it made me feel loved.

But I haven't told you anything about the humorous side of my dad; the side that teaches us every situation has the potential to be funny. Here are some of his views:

On a bumper sticker he put on his camper truck:
"Insanity is inherited; you get it from your kids."

On birth control:
"But Eleanor, we haven't gotten to ten yet."

On what he thought Mom should be doing at age 50:
Sitting in the rocking chair he bought for her.
What Mom did: Got a job as Public Affairs Director at a radio station.

On children born out-of-wedlock:
"Eleanor, how could my son bring this child to me without marriage? That baby cannot be a member of this family."
What he did for the child:
Loved him to pieces.

On airplane rides:
"If God had wanted me to fly he would have outfitted me with wings."

On a fishing trip and how it turned out:
Coming through the patio door, still shaking from the excitement of the day, he implored, "Guess what happen to me today? I caught a rabbit casting my fishing line and shot a fish."

On all his children finally leaving home:
"Whew!"

From my mother I learned something altogether different—understanding. I would have to say that Mother is probably the most patient, understanding person I have ever known. She had the gift of letting all of her children be themselves. By this I mean she didn't spend any time telling us to stop this or don't do that. She mostly guided and listened and allowed us to learn about the world through trial and error. Mother never raised her voice at any of us, and of course she never hit us. She was always there to give advice, but never in a threatening or demeaning way. As a result of her gentleness, we were free to explore the world and develop individually.

Whenever I see young mothers today slapping or jerking their children around, or threatening them or being anything but nice in an attempt to control them, I have to resist the urge to tell them there is a better way. I know because I lived it. My mother knew how to treat us and for this I will always be grateful.

I also learned a lot from my mother about male/female relationships. There were times as a child when I thought Mother should have insisted that Daddy not be so strict with us. I can still hear myself, or one of my sisters, pleading with Mother, "Please talk Daddy into changing his mind." But she wouldn't. She wouldn't even attempt it. Now I realize that she respected him enough to let him have a hand in the rearing of his children. I believe she must have known that we would become strong adults, and he would remain the loving father we all believed him to be.

Now that I'm happily married to a wonderful man, I credit both of my parents with setting a good example for the many years I was with them.

Take care of yourself,
Aunt Bonnie

To Danielle from Aunt Barbara

I had mainly wonderful times growing up with Daddy and Mama. However, I had a hard time trying to figure out whether or not we were poor. I was always happy. I remember playing card games, working jigsaw puzzles, playing hopscotch in the summertime and doing the hula-hoop. I don't remember though, ever talking about us having a lot of money. Yet, I remember Daddy and Mom would get whatever we needed. I never realized what 'being poor' meant. Some of my friends and other people told me "you are poor." I wasn't sure what poor was supposed to feel like. I still don't think the way we were brought up defined being poor. What do you think it means? Do you know why it's confusing? Daddy and Mama always worked, made us stay in school, took us to church, paid the bills and carried us to fun places. We were always doing things together. Maybe we should be called something else. Oh, I know. Poor probably has something to do with an income level, not how hard my parents worked.

I do remember when Daddy used to cook popcorn in the big black skillet. He would rotate the skillet with a big top over the gas jet. Suddenly he would lift off the top and popcorn would jump all over the kitchen floor. No eating popcorn off the floor. Hum. Most of it was on the floor. Danielle, I'm glad it comes in a closed bag today, pops in a microwave and never hits the floor.

When I was six years old, my favorite time with Mama was riding the bus to the eye clinic. We would bring along our lunch, a coloring book and crayons. We counted all the red cars passing near the bus, and once at the doctor's office, Mama read me stories and nursery rhymes. I had her all to myself.

I'll never forget the time she spoke at my junior high school assembly about President Kennedy. Mama was the only member on the panel that did not read notes and made all of us laugh at her stories.

Then I became an adult, got married, and had three children. I visited my mom one day in early October. It was so good to see her. She was so full of energy. Time passes too fast when I am with her.

This day we went out to lunch and discussed growing up in our family. I immediately expressed my thoughts.

"I really learned a lot growing up with Daddy," I say happily. "I learned about being honest, loyal, working hard, being nice to people and not taking advantage of anybody."

"Wait a minute," Mama reacts. "I was there too. What did you learn from me?"

"Oh!" I burst out laughing. "You taught me how to stay sane while going through all that stuff."

Today is Mother's Day. I wrote this just for my mother.

> **M** is for that moment you gave life to me.
> **O**ver the years you've seen that life grow.
> **T** is for the precious thoughts I hold of you.
> **H**onor thy mother. It's my pleasure always to;
> **E** is for the everlasting love we share.
> **R**ejoice! The gift of life to me from you is forever true.

Danielle, stretch out both of your arms as far as you can. I love my mother that much!

Call me when you have time,
Aunt Barbara

To Danielle from Uncle Rich

This is a poem I wrote to my father.

I Am You

There once was a man who took interest in me.
For what reason, I could not see.
I was standing my ground within my space,
My convictions were strong and in the right place.
As I talked with my friends, I meant what I said,
My chest held up high, as I tilted my head.
This man called to me, and he said, "I know you!
The strength and the courage and the stand you take true."
I believed him not, as I told him my name.
He said "You are wrong for I know one the same."
I quizzed him for moments, to find no miscue,
He knew my old man, and he thought I was you!

Hang in there,
Uncle Rich

To Danielle from Uncle Arnold
Hey! My Pops is the Greatest

Do you think your dad is the greatest too? As one of my brothers, I like talking quite often with your dad. Many times we talk about our dad, your grandfather Papa Curry. I call my daddy 'Pops' most of the time because I love him. His actions taught me about caring for people.

Family is more important than just about anything else, including money. This is real true most of the time for most of us.

The character traits I picked up from Dad are manifest in my life too. He's very strong, afraid of nothing and no one. He always stands firm in his beliefs. His beliefs pretty much drive him to be himself. He sees life as being either this way or the other way. None of that 'all over the map' stuff for him.

"Just get to the point, man." I can still hear him saying.

My most vivid memory of Dad happened the day we were working together on a fence at our home. Richmond was driving a Volkswagen and ran into the new fence we had just built around the house. Dad actually lifted up the little car as though it were a toy, "so it won't damage the fence," he said.

Whenever you feel down in the dumps, Pops, being a funny guy without even knowing it, has you laughing in seconds. He looks surprised and wonders what's funny. Danielle, your Dad is good at making people laugh too, but he knows it. Hope to hear from you.

Bye for now,
Uncle Arnold

To Danielle from Dad
Mom with a Man-and-a-Half

Look what you started with the questions you asked Mama Curry. Since I know you are a computer kid, I'll be brief. I'll start by defining the word family. These are people whom you did not pick as friends. You definitely do not get to pick your parents. Mine turned out to be pretty good. I'm talking about the parents. While Mom is a central focal point, it was from Dad that I learned about being forceful. When I was little, Dad looked bigger than anybody I knew. And I was right; he was bigger.

"Relax!" was the greatest one word lesson from Mom. "Don't worry," was her second best lesson.

Good thing we have days like Mother's Day. I sent this original verse to Mom on May 9, 1993.

Seldom does the full meaning of 'Mother' fit a person as well as it fits you. You have proven the task of delivering a child is only the beginning of 'Motherhood.' It takes time, endless patience and mountains of understanding to take just one child from birth to adulthood. And as you know in many ways, getting them to adulthood is hardly the end of the journey.

So, on this Mother's Day I bow to your accomplishments as a mother, person and human being.

Brief enough? That's it for now.

Love you,
Dad

To Danielle from Uncle Paul
Loving and Wonderful People

I'm glad to have a chance to tell you about a couple of loving and wonderful people. Mama and Daddy are keen people to learn from who, definitely impacted my life. Here are four lessons I learned from them that might be interesting to you.

Lesson # 1: I learned at a very early age when Mama says "No" to you about something, 99 times out of 100 she doesn't change her mind. I can't remember one time when she did. Later, I realized Mama, having eight kids, wasn't able to say yes to everything she wanted for her children.

"I said no, but I wish it could be yes," seemed to be her motto.

Lesson # 2: Mama did not waste time. She would ask me to do something around the house or make up my bed. She would only ask me one time. If I took too long, she would do it herself. Boy that really used to make me feel bad. Forget about just feeling bad. I could not ask her for anything for the rest of that day. Mama had this look that was unspeakable. She just looked at you like as if to say 'the nerve of that kid.' That lesson became clear. Do whatever Mama asks you to do, and be happy to do it.

Lesson # 3: Ten words you never want Mama to say, "I'm going to tell your Daddy when he gets home." Mama, being an honest woman, always kept her word on this one. No matter how hard you would beg or plead, it was too late. The thought of having to face Dad coming home tired from work and having to deal with a problem child would many times cause tears to run down my face. I would think about running away from home, but realized I'd just have to face the music. And this music was unpredictable. Trust me, the earplugs didn't work. I learned this lesson well. Do what Mama the boss says now and avoid Dad the enforcer later.

Lesson # 4. Have at least one laugh a day. In other words, Mama could be funny and was always good to be around. She made me feel good. She reminded me of the butterfly: she goes wherever she pleases and pleases wherever she goes.

Now for Dad, he was a hard working man. He loved his wife and children more than life itself. Pops would do anything that he considered right for his family. Once our three older sisters had moved out on their own, Pops had these admonishments for us five boys:

"Never use slang or bad language in front of me."

"No hanging with a bunch of boys on a street corner. Somebody will think up something wrong to do. I know I'm right."

"Whatever you do in life, do the best you can do."

"Don't wait for me to tell you to do something; if you see something out of place fix it without being told."

I'll never forget the time Mama fixed Daddy a special dinner of shrimp, steak and collard greens. My Daddy came home from work as hungry as ever. He glanced at the dinner plate prepared just for him.

"Looks good. What did my kids have for dinner?" He asked.

"Hamburgers," Mama said. "We didn't have enough for everybody to have steak."

"Give them my dinner. Nothing is too good for my kids. We all eat the same thing."

That was the last time Mama cooked a special dinner without having enough for Pop's kids.

Can you believe the great love our parents had and still have for us? They are fascinating people. I have to say with much gratitude, I love them very much. They do those unexpected, unfamiliar and rare things that make life seem to sparkle every day.

Good writing to you, Danielle
Hope to see you for the holidays,

To Danielle from Uncle David
My Dad is a Big Man

It was great seeing you at Mama's house Christmas Eve. I couldn't believe you're all grown up and in college. Nope, I'm not going to say time flies, it just seems like it. Mama told me you want to find out about her and Daddy. Here's a few of my thoughts.

My daddy does everything on a big scale. He built a big house. We had more people in our family than anybody in the neighborhood. We always had a lot of food. Daddy would bring home eight oranges and apples, one for each kid. He'd buy two watermelons. Daddy always bought the most toys and put up the biggest Christmas tree too. And the tree had to be real.

When I was little, Daddy was the biggest man I ever saw. He had a big voice and it sounded loud when he talked or laughed. Sometimes it was scary listening to him. He would not let anyone hurt me though. When he picked me up, I'd be high in the air. He had a big chest. His hands seemed gigantic. But when he hugged me, I felt very safe. Daddy bought a big camper. When I was sixteen years old, I remember him driving us from San Mateo, California to Rockville, Maryland. Daddy was a hard working man, but never seemed tired. He reminded me of a big teddy bear, until I grew up and became bigger than him. Most of all he loved Mama and has the biggest heart of anyone I've ever known.

Now Mama is a different story. Even though she is smaller than my dad is, Mother is strong, sure of herself and faces life in a simple way. Mama listens to you, but she's better at telling you stuff about living right. Two of my favorite expressions from her are actually questions to make you think.

First question.

"Are you better, worse or the same?"

Next question.

"Are you bragging or complaining?"

A comment she often says when things seem hopeless that I still don't get is:

"Every good-bye ain't gone and every shut-eye ain't sleep."

She takes care of all of us emotionally. I use to wonder who took care of her. Mama made you do something so you would learn how it's done. She has an amazing sense of humor, even though she tells me I'm the one that says funny things. I really think Mama works too hard. For example, I was having a rough time when I was about twenty years old making my life work out. I called her.

"Hey, Mom," I said. "How are you doing?"

"Fine and still working," she replied, waiting for the next words from me.

"Mama, I think you need to stop working. You have eight grown kids. If we each give you $100 dollars a month, that's $800 dollars." I stopped to catch my breath. "Don't you think you could live off that and quit that job?"

"Who's going to get this money every month?" Mom asked. Then she quickly said, "I better keep working. Just trying to imagine that happening is a stretch."

"Okay, Mom," I said real fast. "Before you hang up, can you spare me twenty dollars?"

My favorite story on Mom, though, happened at the Martin Luther King Community Center one summer. She happened to be tap dancing for charity and all of a sudden she began jumping rope while tap dancing. She did not miss a beat. I thought she was too old to be dancing, and with a jump rope!

She got an encore, came back out, took a bow.

"More, more, more!" the audience yelled.

"Sorry, I only learned one routine." She smiled, bowed and disappeared.

Another thing, Mama is one of the sanest people I ever met. Of course, I admit I only know about forty-nine people by name.

Danielle, take care,
Uncle Dave

▼

CHAPTER 11

REWARDS OF GIVING

Dear Danielle,

I'd like to share a story about serving others. I was appointed with ten women to the Advisory Council for Women in County Government in 1982. Several young women came to me directly for help concerning their careers. Sometimes, their personal lives were brought into our discussions. I listened to them individually and helped guide them in their decision making. I freely gave this time, getting great satisfaction from assisting them. Seeing these women improve their lives was extremely rewarding. Imagine my surprise when twelve of these women organized an honorary dinner for me.

The dinner was held at the Martin Luther King, Jr. Community Center on November 12, 1983. Papa Curry and our children attended. The planners arranged for our children to "roast" me, in addition to the women themselves thanking me publicly for my support. One very special guest that evening was a woman by the name of Nan Bostick. In addition to serving on the Advisory Council for Women, Nan was also a local singer and songwriter. She wrote this song for the occasion.

Too Much Curry in the Roast
by Nan Bostick

Eleanor's a super wife and mother/Always talking' 'bout her family/so what do they do to show their gratitude?/They turn around and roast her publicly/I'd say there's...
CHORUS:
Too much curry in the roast/too much curry in the roast/too much curry, there's too much curry/there's too much curry in the roast.
(END OF CHORUS)
Eleanor's a spiritual woman/I can tell you God is on her side/Late last night as I was working on this/The Lord came to me and did confide/He said there's...
(REPEAT CHORUS)
Now Eleanor's a fabulous cook/All her friends and relatives will agree/She could make a million bucks if she wrote a cookbook/But just between you and me/I'd say there's...
(REPEAT CHORUS)
Have you heard about her latest money scheme?/She's always dreaming she'll be rich some day/But you and I know if she ever made a bundle/She'd turn around and give it away/You know there's...
(REPEAT CHORUS)
There is one thing, the KSOL van/It's for everyone who works at the station/But no one gets to drive it 'cuz Curry keeps the keys/She's guilty of van confiscation/They say there's
(REPEAT CHORUS, substitute with *too much curry in the van*)
When her back started giving her that trouble/the station called her doctor every day/Saying: Tell her it's our van that's causing' her back pains!/Did she give the van up? No way!/Because there's
(REPEAT CHORUS)
Eleanor's a leader in our struggle/To make this world a better place to be/So we better make some money off of roasting' this fine lady/Or she'll question our integrity!/Because there's...
(REPEAT CHORUS)

After the dinner, the women still felt they wanted to find some way to further thank me. They contacted Bill Somerville, Executive Director of the Peninsula Community Foundation, and suggested starting a scholarship fund in my name. Mr. Somerville said he thought it to be a good idea. I felt honored and welcomed the challenge. I say challenge because it involved me coming up with the first $5,000 dollars to fund the scholarship. Mr. Somerville agreed to match that amount.

I decided to make and sell caftans to raise the money. I spent the next five months at my sewing machine. I made caftans of every color and variety I could think of. Finally there was $3,000.in the bank. Friends came to the rescue and donated the remaining amount of $2,000. December 11, 1986, I took Mr. Somerville the check and he matched it dollar for dollar. Since its inception, the *Curry Scholarship Fund for Girls and Young Women* has assisted several hundred women in pursuing their higher education goals.

Love,
Mama Curry

CHAPTER 12

▼

THE HOUSE THAT LOVE BUILT

Dear Danielle,

Before you were born, we lived in the biggest duplex in San Mateo. Here is a peek at how we came to live there and some memorable moments during our time spent there.

33 North Fremont

The Mustard Seed Man. Do you know who we call the Mustard Seed Man? Papa Curry! "If you have the faith of a tiny mustard seed, you can move mountains," Papa Curry always said.

Faith is about believing. Papa Curry believed he could and promised to build us a house. He did not give an exact date. Yet he had the faith it could happen. We moved to San Francisco in 1955. Ten years later in 1965, with one teenage daughter, one teenage son and four younger sons still living at home, we bought a small two-bedroom house, one bathroom on the first floor and a big dilapidated attic on the second floor. After several attempts to renovate this house, Papa Curry decided it was a hopeless situation. What can we do?

"We'll build a two-bedroom house in the back first, then a garage that I can build a large upstairs rumpus room on top of so the boys can sleep up there," Papa Curry said. Further explaining his vision, "Then we'll tear down the one we're in now and build the main house. I only have one problem."

"What's that?" I asked, getting interested.

"We need a few thousand dollars to buy the blueprints and take them to the Planning Commission."

"I can handle that part," I replied. Getting excited, I continued, "I have a background in designing blueprints for houses." Late most evenings we'd sketch the plans. Weeks later the blueprints were ready.

Everybody had a task. Papa Curry, who was working for a building company, would go to his regular job from eight in the morning until four-thirty in the afternoon, Monday through Friday. He started building the back unit in the evenings and on weekends. The two oldest teenage sons, Richmond and Arnold, worked right alongside their father after dinner. Bill, your dad, at ten years old, took pictures of the construction at various stages. Paul and David, the two youngest sons were taught to sweep up the yard and keep all the debris away from the work site.

Finally, the back apartment was ready to be painted. Close friends brought meatballs and spaghetti, salad, drinks and paint brushes. Before the weekend was over the painting was complete.

Three days later we moved into the spanking brand new apartment. The five sons moved upstairs and named their new living quarters "The Penthouse." After that venture, we all stopped to catch our breath.

Almost ten weeks later the old dilapidated front house was torn down. Once the debris was removed, suddenly it seemed as though we had an extra long front yard, with our apartment far back from the sidewalk. Some of the neighbors wondered what was wrong with us. Two guys were walking down our street one day. I overheard their conversation.

"Hey, that guy must have a loose screw," one man said. "Look how far back from the street he built his house."

"Maybe he doesn't know what he's doing." The other guy said.

"Do you think we ought to tell him we won't bite him?"

"Not me. Have you seen that guy's hands? I'm not saying one word to him."

Others walked by, glancing at the long expanse of land in front of our home and just laughed.

The spring weather was once again good for building and Papa Curry started on the front house. The plans for the main house called for three bedrooms and two bathrooms. A fourth, smaller room, was designated as my sewing room, or be used as a bedroom. The living room had a stone fireplace from its base to the ceiling. Between the two houses was a large two-car garage. We were overwhelmed with the majesty and beauty of both units. A ten-foot lemon tree stood in the front lawn. The front porch steps were graced with a beautiful wrought iron railing. Another most enjoyable sight was the large plate-glass window in the front room of the main house. The exterior was painted sunshine yellow with white trim. The back apartment had a patio, and the front house had a long back porch. I could hardly contain myself due to the splendor put into this house that became our home.

When both units were finally completed and I walked into the various rooms, I was breathless gazing at the beautiful interior. Every room was spacious, built with love from the Mustard Seed Man to his family.

We lived at 33 North Fremont in this serene atmosphere for more than eighteen years. We rented the back unit to Barbara, her husband and their three children. After they moved out, Brenda, our oldest daughter and her three children moved into the apartment. When David finally became an adult, he called 33 North Fremont "the energy field."

My favorite spot inside the main house was the red carpet that went from the front entryway down a hallway that ran the length of the house. Family portraits and certificates of appreciation I had received over the years hung the length of this hallway wall. Visitors loved viewing this section of our home.

We attended many social events at the local Dr. Martin Luther Jr. Community Center while living on North Fremont. It was located just two blocks from our home. We attended the annual Flair's Fall Fling dance for several years. Flair's Dance was held at the Hilton Hotel. Several of our adult children and their mates attended too. I completed college, joined a group of political women in government and helped elect women to governmental positions. We, like most parents, struggled with the world of our teenagers. We were confronted with the "terrible teen" years and "peer pressure" dilemmas. We managed to get the kids through the competitiveness of high school, into higher education, such as trade schools and colleges. They became responsible young adults. One of our best accomplishments has been preparing our eight children to be self-sufficient, loyal and able to earn a decent living. Brenda became a psychologist. Bonnie is a professional writer. Barbara retired from IBM and makes quilts for a hobby. Richmond has many talents is mainly an interior decorator. Arnold is a computer engineer. Bill is a Real Estate broker. Paul and David work in the building trade like Papa Curry. This could not have been possible without God's direction.

Danielle, I need to tell you about the most difficult experience we ever had and how we overcame it. It was a normal sunny morning in October, nothing unusual. Someone rang our doorbell with a letter, but not from the post office. I took the letter and turned it over. I saw a brand new word: FORECLOSURE!

I wondered what that meant. The previous year, Papa Curry had opened the Curry Construction Company and hired two laborers. On the very first contract, the renovation of a local church, his bid was too low. Once into the inner structure of the building, Papa Curry ascertained that an additional high beam needed to be installed. This discovery greatly expanded the original cost. We had made every attempt to secure a new loan from the bank. Loan denied.

We decided to sell our house. But there were no buyers. We realized we were in a jam. I tried to stay focused, that proved to be impossible. When a subpoena was served on me directly, I was non-pulsed. What did the San Francisco courts want? What did I do? Come to find out, 33 North Fremont had been sold to someone from the Fiji Islands. Since we were still living in the house, the potential owner was suing the real estate agent for fraudulent behavior. The house was salable after all. But it was too late for us to save our house. Swiftly a string of foreign words became part of my every day vocabulary: negative cash flow, garnished wages, balloon payment, bankruptcy and subpoena. This was the jargon of the courts and attorneys, the latter, which I had to hire.

Danielle, once again, I was exposed to the strength of Papa Curry. He had to release the two laborers due to lack of funds. Guess what he did? He stayed on the job to complete the task without any monetary reward. He worked daily from February through October, focusing only on getting the job done. At the time, this astonished me. Your dad and uncles came in September to help finish the renovation. A year later, the entire experience had left me drained. I no longer felt strong, able to solve problems, or in control. I felt like I was lost in some deep hole. I was void of feeling any attachment to this catastrophe. Papa Curry found a therapist to help me untangle the web of conflicting emotions I was experiencing in this period of my life. We no longer owned 33 North Fremont. We lost the house and were forced to find another place to live. We rented a modest three-bedroom home in Foster City before purchasing the home we live in today.

Finally, months later, darkness had turned to light. I found an attorney with the most unusual name: Michael Comfort. I perceived this as a message from God. Comfort! I certainly needed to be comforted at that time.

Did anything different come from that avalanche experience? Oh yes. Your dad studied real estate and prepared a pamphlet on Foreclosure to help other families avoid similar circumstance.

While three of your uncles ended up in trades connected to home construction, your two aunts, Bonnie and Barbara, both remodeled their own homes. Their artistic side fully blossomed, allowing them to do such things as design their homes' interiors, sew curtains and drapes, and design and construct beautiful quilts. The major thing that happened to me was turning back to God. No more "Lone Ranger Christianity" for me. How could I pray alone, seldom go to church, and actually believe God was blessing me? After all, God's word says, "Remember the Sabbath day to keep it holy." This I must do according to His word. I joined the local church in our neighborhood. I gave my life back to God and the burdens of my heart rolled away. Praise God! It is good to have peace.

Love you,

Mama Curry

PART III

▼

VIPs

CHAPTER 13

▼

"HAVE YOU MET ANY CELEBRITIES?"

Dear Danielle,

When you hear the word celebrity, whom do you normally think of? Oprah Winfrey comes to mind quickly. Of course we think of other entertainers, sports figures, musical divas, politicians or anyone doing the latest incredible thing. The list could include national leaders, media personalities and motivational speakers, too. There have been many celebrities who have had a positive influence on my life. Some of them I've met personally. Others whom I have not met are included here because of the profound effect they have had on me just knowing of their contributions to society. They're also included because I want you to keep in mind that we never know how another's acts of compassion will touch us, teach us, and move us to do great things ourselves. In the following pages are some of my more memorable encounters with some the celebrities I have met.

Wally Amos
Entrepreneur, Motivational Speaker

From 1995 to 2000, I served as president of the African American Community Entrustment, a fundraising partner of the United Way of the Bay Area. We chose to honor grandmothers because of the love and dedication they have always shown to children. The keynote speaker at our very first *Honoring Grandmothers* awards dinner was Wally (Famous) Amos. He can best be described as intriguing. In sharing with the audience how his grandmother taught him to make that famous cookie, Wally's positive mental attitude captivated the audience. Yet my favorite time with him happened on our way to lunch one day. We were walking down Market Street in San Francisco. A guy behind us was wearing a watermelon cap, watermelon vest and watermelon tennis shoes. A woman coming from the opposite direction stared at him and said, "You look disgusting."

We turned around, looking at the guy. The guy said to the woman.

"Hey, lady," he said yawning, without a misstep. "Whatever you think of me is none of my business." Wally and I laughed deciding the guy was right.

At one time, Wally was one of the top fifty motivational speakers in the country. He is the author of two of my favorite books, *The Power Within You* and *Man Without A Name*. In those books he writes about how he believes anyone can overcome any negative challenges, even strangers making unsolicited comments.

Maya Angelou
Poet

In 1994, the Spring Foundation arranged to have Maya Angelou as their keynote speaker. I was chosen to be her escort for the day. When I arrived at the Park Hotel in Palo Alto to pick her up, she was having her breakfast. I told the receptionist to let her know I would be waiting in the lobby for her.

"Ms. Angelou wants you to join her," the receptionist said.

"Thank you." I moved toward her table. "Hello, Ms. Angelou," I said. Then I became speechless.

"Sit down." She was completely relaxed. "Had breakfast yet?"

I didn't know what to say. Finally I uttered, "I am a little nervous being here with you, alone."

"You'll get over it," she smiled. "Order some food and the bubbles will go away."

I took her advice and ordered juice and toast. Ms. Angelou's easy going manner and natural calm did much to soothe my jitters that day.

Ms. Angelou was on stage that day for almost two hours. Her words were electrifying; including her reading, *And Still I Rise*, one of her more widely read and recited poems.

Danielle, please read *I Know Why the Caged Bird Sings* by Maya Angelou. It's an excellent book and well worth your time. You should also know that Ms. Angelou became the first black writer to read one of her poems at a presidential inauguration. That was in 1993 when William Clinton first took office. She wrote the poem entitled *On the Pulse of Morning* especially for this occasion. It too is well worth the read.

Chuck Berry
Entertainer

One of my claims to fame was having known Chuck Berry, the Father of Rock & Roll. He lived in St. Louis, where he and your grandfather were good friends as teenagers. The guys used to tease Chuck because he played his guitar all the time. Some of them would try to beat him up and break his guitar. Papa Curry would chase them away. They remained good friends until Chuck left St. Louis, made many hit records and traveled all over the world.

Chuck was on tour in California in 1978. I happened to be working at KSOL Radio at that time. We went to see him perform at the Circle Stare Theatre in San Carlos. When Earl asked to see Chuck before he went on stage, the security guard said that was not possible. Earl wrote his name on a slip of paper and asked the guard to give it to Chuck. The guard took the piece of paper and disappeared backstage. He returned just a few moments later and escorted us to Chuck's dressing room. They had not seen each other for thirty-two years. The two men embraced, overcome with emotions.

"Man, where in the world have you been?" Chuck asked. He was obviously glad to see his old friend.

"I've been watching you perform all over the world," Earl replied. "I got married and had a house full of kids like my Dad." They both laughed.

Chuck went on stage moments later and dedicated his hit, *Sweet Little Sixteen,* to Papa Curry. Near the end of his performance Chuck asked, "Will Earl Curry please stand up?" Chuck explained to the crowd, "He's a buddy from way back." Over a dozen men stood up, but not Papa Curry. Chuck hollered, "Sit down. Hey Earl, stand up." Earl finally stood up. Everybody clapped and cheered.

After the show was over, many people crowded around Papa Curry asking him for his autograph because he knew Chuck Berry.

Mary McCleod Bethune
Entrepreneur, College Founder

I mentioned Mary McCleod Bethune in an earlier letter to you—when I was discovering important people through my studies of Negro history in high school. Miss Bethune impressed me because she was featured in an article in *Ebony* magazine. Imagine a woman who taught children how to write by squeezing the juice out of a beet to use as ink then writing words on toilet paper.

Miss Bethune was president of the National Congress of Negro Women. She was a key member of President Franklin D. Roosevelt's "Black Cabinet" advisers. After he was elected in 1932, the Black

Cabinet advised President Roosevelt on racial issues in our country. Danielle, I was only four years old when Miss Bethune's services became vital to our people. At that time, she was the Founder and President of Bethune-Cookman College and Director of the Negro Affairs Division/National Youth Administration. Later, when the United Nations was established in San Francisco in 1945, Mary McCleod Bethune was one of the American observers attending the conference. Her legacy remains alive today through the National Council of Negro Women. Her legacy, which influenced my growth, remains very much a part

Barry Bonds
Baseball Player

I first met Barry Bonds while serving on the Bay Area United Way Board of Directors. Barry was also on the Board, giving generously of his time and resources. Through his generosity, computers were made available to low-income children in the cities of East Palo Alto and Oakland. Barry also helped to open a Bone Marrow Registry in the African American community to assist persons in need of transplants. Acts like these, performed without fanfare or the media looking on, are the true measure of a man's character.

I have had the pleasure of meeting Barry's mother, Pat Bonds, at a United Way Board of Directors luncheon. At first I thought she was his sister; due to her youthful look. After being introduced and informed that she was his mother, I was somewhat taken aback. Pat is a balanced, gracious, refined person. I have since enjoyed working with her on several non-profit projects. She is a key team member, for example, supporting our annual *Honoring Grandmothers Awards* event with the African American Community Entrustment in 1996. While we have heard many stories about Barry's father, Bobby, his mother was equally important in developing Barry's character. Her best advice, "Stick to one thing at a time and do it exceedingly well."

My most famous memory of Barry happened when he hit his seventy-third home run in 2001 (on my seventy-third birthday). My memories are many and precious when it comes to his mom, Pat.

Dr. Martin Luther King, Jr.
Minister, Civil Rights Leader

While I have never met Dr. King personally, Papa Curry and I attended the Montgomery Bus Boycott Rally held at the San Francisco Cow Palace in 1960. Dr. King spoke about the value of being a disciple of nonviolence in the quest for social justice. He became famous on the national level when Ms. Rosa Parks refused to give up her seat on the front of the bus in the South. She refused to go to the back of the bus. She was arrested, and her arrest spearheaded the bus boycott. Dr. King, in response, stepped forth, preaching against segregation and the damage racism inflicts upon society. It was A. Philip Randolph, president of the Brotherhood of Sleeping Car Porters, who organized the historical 1963 March on Washington. However, it was Dr. King who electrified the entire country with his *I Have a Dream* speech.

Danielle, on the day of that speech I was sitting in my living room, trying to remain cool when Dr. King began to speak. Just imagine for a moment witnessing a black man on television engaging the attention of millions of people for the very first time in history. He received the Nobel Peace Prize for the nonviolent movement he initiated and became known as the leader of the Civil Rights Movement.

After he was assassinated in 1968, I met his wife, Coretta Scott King, in 1976 in Monterey, California. Hundreds of us came from miles around to stand in a long receiving line waiting to greet her. Mrs. King appeared serene and very peaceful.

"How can you be so tranquil and kind, yet not bitter?" I asked.

"We knew his life would be taken," she replied. "We didn't know when. We know also he is in heaven."

Danielle, Dr. King's very name evokes unbelievable actions from citizens around the world. This is the first time in the history of the

United States we have a national holiday honoring a black leader. During this historical period, when Dr. King was spearheading change across this land, at the local level many of us were marching to make precise things take place as well. We followed his lead and tried to right some of the wrongs that had been administered upon so many for so long. Here are some of the issues a host of others and I was directly involved in implementing:

Broadcasting a series on KSOL-Radio entitled the *Life and Works of Dr. Martin Luther King, Jr.*

Organizing an annual parade in San Francisco with Glide Memorial Church

Demonstrating to have the name of the local community center in San Mateo renamed King Community Center

Sponsoring the North Central Neighborhood Association Annual Essay *Contest* to encourage youth in the literary field

Awarding scholarship to local students

Co-sponsoring a rally with the Martin Luther King School in San Francisco along with his son, Martin Luther King, III

All of these events, as well as many other events by people we don't even know, were the direct result of how Dr. Martin Luther King, Jr. inspired so many to do so much.

Joe Louis
Professional Boxer

Long before there was a Mike Tyson or a Muhammad Ali, there was a Joe Louis (the Brown Bomber). Here was a man who started his boxing career in 1934 when racism still permeated many parts of the country. He had won the heavyweight boxing title in 1937 and successfully defended that title twenty-five times. This was at a time when there was no television (it hadn't been invented yet) so most of the Negroes across the country gathered around radios to hear the action whenever he fought. We knew what Joe Louis looked like from seeing his pictures in newspapers and magazines. We never dreamed we'd ever see him in person.

In the late 1940s, Aunt Rosa, Papa Curry's older sister, and Charles Abernathy, her husband, owned the Deluxe Hotel in St. Louis. We worked there from time to time doing various duties assigned to us. Many famous Negroes of the day stayed at the Deluxe when they traveled to St. Louis. Segregation was still a social reality, a condition enforced by the law. Weary Negro travelers, rich and middle class, chose the Deluxe Hotel as their favorite place to stay.

One warm summer day in 1947, Joe Louis came to town. Excitement was high among the dozen people on the staff. Toni, a tiny four-foot, nine-inch waitress, was determined to get an autograph. All of us wanted his autograph. But Toni was the only one with a plan.

"I'm going right up to him and say, 'Hi, Mr. Louis, sign right here.'" Joe Louis arrived in a tiny Volkswagen driven by his bodyguard. Suddenly a throng of people outside the hotel appeared from every direction. Toni squeezed through the crowd, ran to the car. Just as the car door opened, Joe Louis stepped out. Toni looked up at him, and up, and up, and up. He was well over six feet tall. Toni stood there staring and voiceless. Joe Louis smiled and started signing whatever was thrust in front of him. Many others gathered around vying for his autograph. Toni was lost in the shuffle. Joe Louis graciously signed autographs for quite some time. I was in awe by his graciousness with ordinary people. After all, he was the Brown Bomber. But he was also kind and a gentleman. He even acknowledged the "tiny" Toni by giving her an autograph once he had come inside.

Jackie Robinson
Baseball Player

Jackie Robinson was the first African American to enter major league baseball. The year was 1947. Like Joe Louis, Jackie often stayed at the Deluxe Hotel whenever he played in St. Louis. People would jam the premises whenever they heard he was in town. Many wanted to look at him, touch him, take pictures with him or just shout out his name. We had to bring him through a secret entrance, as the number of fans who always showed up was astonishing. Although he was a strong man, he had to be protected from the crowds. He was extremely intelligent, sensitive and a perfect gentleman. He always thanked the staff for "extending such kindness..." We were thrilled to be at his service.

As segregation was coming to end, white hotels opened their facilities to the general public, regardless of color. Many of our customers started patronizing businesses on the other side of town, following the celebrities like Jackie Robinson into those businesses. Business at the Deluxe Hotel dropped so low the owners were forced to sell the building. Unfortunately, the change in the segregated laws left too many Negro businesses unprepared for this dramatic drop in business, and many closed. Yet, on the other hand, segregated living was not financially good for us either. So while we experienced liberation on the one hand, unexpected 'lack of money' struggles, fostered new woes on the other.

This shift made people in the black community begin to think about seeking employment and other opportunities in the community at large. You have to remember that during the 1930s and 1940s blacks and whites did not live, work, or socialize together. I'll say again, as a youngster and a young adult, I rarely if ever saw anybody white. My entire world was made up of black people. Seeing people like Jackie Robinson and Joe Louis, icons to all of us, go into the broader community and enjoy success, had a profound effect on most of us.

Eleanor Roosevelt
First Lady of the United States

Although I have never met her, Eleanor Roosevelt heavily influenced my thinking. She was the wife of the thirty-second president of the United States, Franklin D. Roosevelt. My mother greatly admired her, too, naming me after her. She was a leader and a symbol of the people who struggled for freedom. I studied her philosophy. I remember learning that right after the Great Depression of 1929, many people could not find jobs and most people did not have enough food to feed their families. In what has become known as the "New Deal," President Roosevelt established fifteen new legislative initiatives, one that enabled millions of jobless people to find work. He also rationed out food to those in need. We were by that time near starvation. Can you believe we received the food that was rationed, too? We were overjoyed at seeing so much food. Mother told me that was one reason people loved President Franklin D. Roosevelt. My love for Mrs. Roosevelt also stems from my knowledge of her willingness to take a stand on controversial issues. An example of this can be seen in an incident that happened in 1939.

When the Daughters of the American Revolution (DAR) refused to allow Marian Anderson (one of the greatest classically trained singers of the twentieth century who just happened to be African American) sing at Constitution Hall in Washington, D.C., it created uproar. Mrs. Roosevelt resigned from the DAR and arranged for Marian Anderson to instead sing at the Lincoln Memorial on Easter Sunday. Over 75,000 people attended the performance. The message of support from this gesture left an enormous impression on me. This proved more dramatic than starting a war.

Gloria Steinem
Feminist

Many years ago (1978), I wrote a weekly column for the now defunct *Peninsula Bulletin* newspaper. The late Charles Thrower, the newspaper's editor at that time, assigned me the task of interviewing Gloria Steinem. I was asked to find out her thoughts on women's issues. He especially wanted to know if her thoughts had any relevance to black women's issues. Through prior arrangements, members of the press were invited to a press conference at Stanford University to meet with Steinem. We were ushered into a private room at Stanford on the appointed date. As we entered, there sat this tiny woman with long, wheat colored hair and eyeglasses so huge they dwarfed her tiny 100-pount frame. Her smile was magnetic and genuine. Immediately I thought, '*What in the world can she know about black women's issues*'? The large number of men in attendance also struck me. The topic was *Women and Wealth.*

Steinem talked about poor and middle class women having to work out of necessity, while rich women may lead privileged lives and still be extremely deprived regarding the subject of money. It appeared very clear that white women may have access to large sums of money. In reality it was the men who actually controlled the finances—as husbands, brothers, uncles, or professional male counterparts. I realized why so many men were present. This press conference pointed to emerging women who threatened a shift in the financial affairs of men, a shift to rich women. After tremendous applause as she finally told the women who were attending to 'Go and do something outrageous.'

Walking outside the auditorium, I was mentally rehashing Steinem's revolutionary speech about the role of feminists, be they women or men. Ms. Steinem had mentioned, for example, that one of the traveling team members, Attorney Florynce (Flo) Kennedy, had taken the position strong positions on certain views about abuse. One doesn't have to accept the opposition's terms.' These conversations triggered the depth of domestic violence and incest prevailing in this country. If you talk to any group of five to six women, one of them has probably been abused. I met

Attorney Flo Kennedy personally, at Canada College, in Redwood City, California. I reported back to Mr. Thrower.

"Yes, Gloria Steinem has a message about black women's issues, and she boldly exposes issues of inequality. She respects us for identifying such issues ourselves, whether we are black, white or of any other color facing inequities."

Gloria Steinem, founding editor of *New York* magazine and political columnist until 1971, was also one of the founders of the *Ms Foundation* for women. So in 1978, as we strolled along, deep in our own personal thoughts after leaving Stanford University, we begin talking again.

"What do you plan to do that's outrageous?" My friend asked, breaking our silent walk.

"I've been doing something outrageous already for the last thirty some odd years."

"What have you been doing?" She looked puzzled.

"Staying married." My friend laughed, confessing she had done the same thing and declaring, "We're going to become very good friends."

Willie Brown
Politician

Anyone near the San Francisco political arena has a story about former Mayor Willie Brown. One day in 1980 he came to KSOL to participate in a radio program. At that time he was assembly speaker in Sacramento, and not yet mayor. When he arrived, he had to produce the program immediately in order to get to his next appointment. We had a preliminary review of the questions I would be asking. Once we began the program I asked him the first question. Ten minutes later (mind you now, we were on the air) Mayor Brown was still talking.

"Now that we've covered the budget, I can tell you about the next plans," he said. During thirty minutes of airtime, I only asked two questions. Then the program was over. The public called asking us to repeat this program a dozen times. Our ratings went through the roof.

Once he became the mayor of San Francisco, the first *Women's Summit* was held. Mayor Brown insisted that scholarships be made available for young women and teenagers. At the very first conference he stayed the entire day. He listened attentively to women from throughout the nation. Hey, Danielle! I just remembered something. You were there with Mindy and me as one of the students from San Mateo County. I remember you telling me afterward, "That was awesome." This is an example of how dynamic a leader Willie Brown is and how supportive he is of women.

One of my favorite stories about Willie Brown, though, happened when the Pope came to town. The line of dignitaries waiting to be introduced to the Pope included Clint Eastwood and Speaker Willie Brown. As the Monsignor was making introductions, here's what happened.

"Your Honor, this is." the Monsignor hesitated, completely forgetting Clint Eastwood's name. He tried again, "This is, ah…" The Pope quickly interrupted, "That's Dirty Harry."

The next day, Speaker Brown was in line standing next to the Pope at city hall in San Francisco. A homeless bag lady was standing in line hoping to see Speaker Brown. A well dressed, upper-middle class woman was also standing in line just behind the bag lady. She looked through her binoculars and asked her friend, "Who's that man in the long white cape?"

The bag lady responded, "I don't know who the man in the cape is, but the man standing next to him, that's Assembly Speaker Willie Brown."

Anna Eshoo
Congresswoman

Anna Eshoo represents the 14th Congressional District in California. I met her in Redwood City in 1983 when she was running for a seat on the San Mateo County Board of Supervisors. She won the election. One of our fondest memories happened a few years later in 1987. Remember the earlier letter about Viola White sending my name to an awards committee at the *San Francisco Foundation*. The award I received was the prestigious *Foundation Award for Contributions to the Improvement of Human Relations in the Bay Area*. Supervisor Eshoo presided at the proceedings when the award was presented to me. She said to the crowd of over three hundred, "Eleanor Curry is the first person in a twenty-five-year period to be recognized by the Foundation in our county. She is one of our most valued, most treasured human beings." Most recently, after I had given a speech at the *Women's Hall of Fame* 20th *Anniversary* celebration, a copy of my speech was sent to Congresswoman Eshoo. She sent me this response:

Dear Eleanor,

I just sat down and read your piece, The Triple "V's": Values, Virtuous and Victorious. It is magnificent and you are magic. You never cease to amaze me, teach me, and inspire me.

How blessed we all are to have you ennobling our lives and our community. How especially blessed I am to call you my friend.

My love for always,
Anna Eshoo

Donna Chestang Jackson
Police Officer and Radio Personality

The saying goes, "To let your light so shine that people become spellbound when they suddenly see you." Donna Chestang Jackson does spellbind people, yet she is totally oblivious to her magnetic glow. The magic happened to me when this five-foot, four-inch woman walked into my office at KSOL Radio. When several job openings came up at KSOL, Donna was hired for one of the positions. She had already served as a police officer for ten years on the Oakland Police Force. In addition to her responsibilities as a peace officer, Donna would drive the forty miles from Oakland to San Mateo each week to produce a talk show entitled *Crime, the Courts and You.* Later she chose to become my assistant in Public Affairs. By 1990, it was time for me to make another career move. Once Donna was fully prepared to manage Public Affairs, we offered her the challenge. She was an instant celebrity. Her voice was sharp and loud, yet sensitive and penetrating. Donna said of herself, "I'm not a singer, or a rock star, yet I love being associated with community affairs."

What about her shining light? Donna had a unique sense of style and her personality radiated like a bright daytime star. Once, for example, the two of us went shopping on a hot summer day. We stopped to get a cold drink in a small restaurant. The clerk was smitten with Donna. She was wearing a lemon green shift and ponytail. He poured the coke all over the counter—twice—staring at Donna. He found his voice, asking me, "Are you this lady's agent?"

"No. Are we ever going to get a coke?" I asked jokingly.

On another hot day we went to lunch in Walnut Creek and attempted to cross the busiest street at the Mall. Suddenly a truck driver parked his vehicle in the intersection and beckoned us to cross as he released a low respectful whistle.

Another time we were together in church for Sunday morning services when a little boy about the age of seven stared at Donna then
peeped under her hat. The child turned asking his mother, "Mommy,
can I go sit by that pretty lady?" We never know the full effect of
Donna's outer glow. After coming in contact with hundreds of
interns and volunteers, Donna stands out from the crowd. She has an
uncanny ability to pick up a story before it becomes state or national
news. An example of this happened when she met with the Oakland,
California mother who began the "Just Say No" campaign during an
interview on KSOL. Months later, after visiting Oakland schools,
First Lady Nancy Reagan made it a popular rallying cry for the
anti-drug movement.

Donna enjoyed working with young people, from second graders
to the college bound hopefuls. Whenever she spoke to teenagers, she
had an unusual message concerning current events. Right near the
end of her presentation Donna would ask, "Anybody here having a
birthday today?" Once hands would go up, Donna would say, "Let's
sing happy birthday to you right now." After the singing ended,
Donna would say, "Now come on down here and get a voter registra-
tion card. When you turn eighteen, get ready to register to vote and
you'll be somebody."

How can I describe Donna and how she lives her life in twenty
words or less? She is daughter, sister, and wife, single mother, police
officer, radio personality, volunteer, computer whiz, Christian, best
friend, and even plays the piano. Donna continues to shine and mes-
merize. Donna Chestang Jackson received a Liberal Arts Degree from
Holy Name College Oakland, California, May 2001. She keeps
inspiring me, others, and surprising herself.

Claire Mack
City Mayor, Community Activist

My good friend Claire Mack has accomplished many great things
in the political arena of San Mateo. She became the first black mayor
in San Mateo's 100-year history on December 5, 1994. Prior to her

victory, she had been the Public Affairs Director for KCSM, a college television station at the College of San Mateo. KCSM aired a daily program that showcased local issues, a venue that allowed Claire to raise awareness on a broad range of community topics.

Claire hated to see anything she considered out of order. When graffiti began appearing in our neighborhoods, for example, Claire formed a team of young workers and started cleaning it off the walls. Every spot either got scrubbed off or painted over.

While on the City Council for twelve years, she fought passion-ately to make the neighborhood called North Central in San Mateo as fabulous as the rest of the city. This meant no dumping grounds, cheap housing, homeless shelters or soup kitchens in North Central. "Such social services should not be next door to people's homes," Claire argued. She was successful in keeping them out.

Claire is blessed with a caring spirit and a heart of gold. She baked specialty cakes to make extra money to donate to those in need. She went to the King Community Center to help her neighbors plan for such events as the city's 100th birthday party. Her lists of achieve-ments are as varied as her viewpoints. She has been a businesswoman, a playwright, a poet and a television and radio host on KGO Radio and KCSM TV. Claire has served on the San Mateo County Grand Jury, as well as on numerous city and school district advisory boards and commissions. For well over twenty-five years, the residents of San Mateo have greatly benefited from Claire's tirelessness and ability to get things done.

Ruth Nagler
Community Activist

The first school board meeting I ever attended was at the San Mateo Elementary School District in 1966. I witnessed this 5-foot 2-inch woman on the School Board holding her own with four male Board members. I sat fascinated at her skill in getting her points across, voting her mind and not getting shoved aside. I knew I wanted to know her better. I'd like you to know about her, too. First, one of the major things I found out that night was how to shake hands with a very firm grip. Mine was rather limp or hesitant; hers was firm and direct.

Her backup was Ed Nagler, her husband who had attended nearly every Board meeting with her. Ed came into focus one night when the subject was extremely controversial. The room was jammed with middle-class parents upset over a school closure. Ruth was the Chairperson of the San Mateo Elementary School Board. I wondered if she would survive all the hostility emanating from the angry parents. Suddenly a voice from the back of the room shouted, "Give 'them Hell, Ruth!" It was Ed.

Ruth was a shrewd judge of character. She was an authority on establishing, strengthening and settling things. Her name was connected to any community improvement that would benefit San Mateo County. When she was the Director of the Community Education for the San Mateo County Community College District, for example, Ruth initiated, designed, developed and administered non-credit short courses, conferences, special events and workshops. At this time her services still reach more than 48,000 people. The range of diverse topics offered throughout San Mateo County is the direct result of Ruth Nagler's efforts.

Ruth, as a volunteer, promoted causes for the common good she believed to be important. Here are some of causes for which she has volunteered:

Trustee and a key leader, San Mateo Elementary School Board;
Coordinator of *San Mateo County 2000* for the Public Library System
Chairperson of the Friends of the Advisory Council on Women
Member of the Mills-Peninsula Hospital Board of Trustees
Member of the League of Women Voters
Chairperson of the San Mateo Performing Arts Center, Board of Directors
Chairperson of the Center for the American Musical

The private side of Ruth is equally dynamic. She and Ed raised two sons, Michael and Dave, and she enjoys two grandchildren. She has an unparalleled sense for determining when things need to be changed, enjoyed or left alone. Ruth is also famously known for her fabulous mid-day parties where we could always find a mixture of exciting and interesting guests. How did Ruth handle this massive volume of activities that would cause most of us to become immobilized? Frankly, I think, Ruth is really two people.

Jackie Speier
California State Senator, 8th District

"What is Jackie Speier like?" Many students have asked that question when I visited local high schools and talked about women's issues. "Do you know her? Is she as nice as she seems? When did you meet her? Does she like girls and women or just politics?"

"Jackie Speier has a strong work ethic," I would begin. "She is symbolic of what a sound education can nearly guarantee a person. She is a Democrat, yet has had 116 bills signed into law by two Republican Governors. But Ms. Speier is not all politics. She is one of the most personable of people persons one could meet. She has an inquisitive mind, an attentive attitude and a ready smile.

I first met Jackie around 1977 when she provided legal counsel to Congressman Leo Ryan. I was on the Education Committee, exploring ways to get teenage girls into West Point Academy. In the Jonestown, Guyana tragedy Congressman Ryan was shot and killed. Jackie was also shot that day, but was fortunate enough to have survived. Shortly thereafter, she became one with all the people who were grief stricken.

I have immense respect for this great woman. I joined Jackie for her first run for public office, when in 1980 she became the youngest elected member of the San Mateo County Board of Supervisors. She was re-elected for a second term and became Chair of the Board in

1985. Three years later, Jackie was the first member of the California Legislature to give birth while in office.

Today she has a teenage son and a younger daughter. Jackie Speier loves children, especially girls. Her Young Women's Health Conference is held annually in San Francisco, now in its fourth year, with more than 1,000 young women attending each year. The Conference is a community collaboration that includes the UCSF National Center of Excellence in Women's Health, the San Francisco Unified School District, health clinics and other organizations serving the youth.

I'm grateful to be such good friends with her. Papa Curry and I had our marriage vows renewed at her private residence in 1994. We are both proud, too, to have State Senator Jackie Speier representing the 8th District in Sacramento, California.

Mildred Swann
Community Activist

Mildred Swann, the wife of Willie Swann, mother of Calvin, Brian and Lynn Swann, plus the matriarch to a large extended family, wears several hats. She's been a gifted leader. Hundreds of parents and teenagers have benefited from her counseling, her guidance toward college and her personal attention. In later years, I interviewed Mildred, focusing on her philosophical thoughts on parents, children and community. Here is our interview:

What do you do?

When? (Mildred smiled. Then she got serious.) Currently, I work for the San Mateo Union High School District, as its Outreach Coordinator. This covers academics, attendance and accessing information, enabling students to prepare for high school campus life, plus informing students of college preparatory requirements.

What is the role of the parents?

It is very different. One of my main tasks is to organize the parents, informing them about the campus, social and community needs of their teenage children. About thirty-five years ago we had three

Latino families in San Mateo. Today we have Asian, Latino, Tongan and African Americans in this district. Too many of these students seem not to fully comprehend the modern day high school atmosphere.

What aspect are they missing?

Top priority is definitely to study and prepare for the future with a skill they have mastered. If one door slams shut, another one opens, so be prepared. When I decided to study to be a dental assistant, despite being discouraged, I kept going. The woman at the trade school told me, "Black people never apply for dental training." I told her not to tell me what I can or cannot do. While they would train her on the job, I will not have the same privilege. I took the course, was prepared and got the job.

Are there any other changes?

Just over the past thirty years, we look at some big changes. Yes, the teenagers need more parental involvement at every level. Take the lack of reading. Mix this with the impact of TV, radio, clothes, music and the songs heard over and over. These habits become imbedded into their minds. Isolation is another struggle, which almost says, "Let's leave it to the kids."

Mildred leaned in, even more serious, opening both hands, then closing them.

Remember when all the families in our neighborhood knew each other? Inside our homes we were eating together. We were taught to say 'good morning' and 'good night.' No such thing as crashing parties. We had to respect everybody. One habit we still enforce is staying in touch. It's easy to just call and let us know you're okay.

What are your thoughts on 'To Spank or not to Spank?'

I believe in spanking the kids. If God had intended for kids not to be spanked, He would not have padded their little bottoms. Of course you should not mistreat the child or abuse the child. A big strong person should never shake a little child or a child of any age. If you use brute force, or strike a child when angry, that's wrong. Today's modern parents are dealing with a new phenomenon called "time out."

Even if time out removes spanking, parents have to be in charge of the process, its duration and enforcement.

Where are you from originally?

Alcoa, Tennessee. I remember the good school life we had, although it was segregated. We had a relationship with the white neighbors, never bringing up racial separation. Yet it was visible to a degree. It was a bit odd to be a part of it, however, it did exist. We could play on their fields and sing in their choirs. We even lived next door to white neighbors. Alcoa, Tennessee happens to be the home of Alcoa Aluminum. My Dad worked there. He had a very prominent position. My grandfather was the owner of the first restaurant and boarding house, in spite of the laws. We somehow understood the rules. The bus had seats, back to back. We automatically figured out where to sit. The town was made up of several types of groups: the rich people, the well to do and those who owned their homes. My father and mother were among the well educated. Freddie, my only and older sister, and I were only one of two families that could take a vacation. We would go to New York.

What do the words Family, Safety, Freedom, Duty and Vote make you think about?

The *family* is very important. God entrusted it to us, to love each other, respect each other and be there. *Safety* is what to look for, especially when selecting true friends. They watch your back. It's critical to learn the do's and don'ts of life. One needs to know how to handle the police officers as allies, not enemies. When we are free within ourselves, *freedom* cannot have any limitations on us. We have the right to set goals, live out our goals without stepping on others to get ahead. Everybody should *vote*. Once you turn eighteen years old, everybody must exercise the right to vote. Too many of our people have died fighting for voting rights. No matter where you live, even in the South, vote. One vote does truly matter. Whether you like the party that wins, just wait and vote again and again. We have taught all our children to register and vote. God comes first when I think about the word duty. I think duty to God, to self and to our country. This is really about respecting ourselves.

Where do we belong?

We belong here! We were brought to this country. We must be respected and treated right in this country. As a people, we are smart. We have every type of great people among the black race. When I went to Africa, I found my descendents. They are Africans. We are Americans of African descent. We belong here!

*   *   *   *

Danielle, Mildred Swann was named the Citizen of the Year, 1994, in San Mateo, due to her local involvement with young people. Her name is engraved in concrete at Mills Hospital on San Mateo Drive and Second Avenue in San Mateo. The evening she was presented this award was an extremely cold night. So cold, in fact, that she arrived at the event in a full-length mink coat. But Mildred's disposition warmed the crowd in spite of the chilly weather.

Dr. Doris Ward
Politician

For over 30 years, Dr. Ward has been a multi-talented, creative, take-charge elected official. The first African American woman to fill the position of County Assessor in San Francisco, Doris transformed the assessor's office from the "most dysfunctional in the state" (according to a 1992 California auditor's report) into a modern, technologically proficient unit of government. Under her leadership, more than one billion dollars in taxes was brought into the city's coffers, increasing the assessed value of city property to eighty-eight billion dollars, the highest amount in San Francisco history.

Doris has been the "first" in many public endeavors. She sponsored an educational youth conference in San Mateo County for high school students. On more than one occasion she planned multicultural training seminars for teachers and administrators. This she did because of her insight into the importance of people from differing backgrounds learning about each other. She served as a recruitment coordinator bringing African American teachers to the Bay Area. She was elected to the Community College Board in San Francisco and has held several positions at the national level.

On the private side, her most dramatic "first" came with the beginning of her "Hen Party," which she began in 1969. That first gathering was just lunch during the Christmas season with three close friends. By the 1990s, it had blossomed into a twenty-four-hour feast including people representing three generations of women and their families arriving around the clock.

Did Doris have any dreams? Yes! She wanted to treat her special friends to a seven-day vacation if she ever became rich enough. Her dream came true for a dozen of us when she saw an opportunity to blend work and pleasure. One day Doris called me, excited and said, "This is as close as I can get to a seven-day vacation. You'll have to work for five of the days, but the rest of the time will be yours. I need a dozen intergroup specialists to help map out a desegregation plan for a school district in a central state. This will be a retreat. Can you do this?" Everyone she asked said yes. We made travel plans and landed in a resort that was heaven. Five days later, the mission was complete. We asked how we would know the end result. Doris told us to listen to the national news. "If it's reported that a central state voted in favor of a desegregation plan, then we've done our job." Sure enough the plan was accepted. We congratulated each other and cheered Dr. Doris Ward.

Celebrity Bosses

Bosses are different kinds of celebrities. They have the power to make or break our career, especially since today people change jobs approximately every seven years or so. The boss is critical to our future in any given career. The key reason we're there is to make the boss look good and to get paid. Always do your best. Forget about just halfway working.

Believe me, bosses see you when you are working. They definitely see you when you are not working. Every time they look your way, make sure you're working. It might happen that once you're on the job for a few months, you start wondering if the boss is as stupid as he is or she appears. Forget that. Focus on what you can learn from a person who seems stupid. I've had more than my fair share of them. They must know something to have reached the position of "Boss."

For anyone who has a job, the boss is a necessary force, whether for good or bad. Did I learn from bosses? Yes! If you look closely, you will find many strengths and weaknesses hidden in their hearts. Then again, some day you might have a boss like I once had, a boss who doesn't seem to be stupid, but who just doesn't do anything. Guess what? That kind of boss always suffers the most, for the hardest thing about doing nothing is not knowing when you're through. Never mind the bosses who do nothing either. That is, never attempt to evaluate anybody who is over you in rank. If you don't know what he or she is doing, well that means you are too busy working to notice the boss. Here are some of the many "celebrity" bosses who have influenced me positively.

Mrs. Bergman
Restaurant Manager

Recall that Mrs. Bergman was the rigid manager of the white middle class restaurant where I first worked as a teenager. This woman was my first boss. She hired most of us when we were as young as fourteen years old to avoid paying higher wages. She was fastidiously funny, all the while intending to be serious. From her we learned the importance of being ready for work and being on time. We learned of speaking only when spoken to. We learned, and were warned, not to flirt with her twenty-year-old son when he came in for dinner. The latter item, though, was not in our job descriptions. This became a side issue that later cost two of the bus girls their jobs. The remaining three of us then quit to support the two who were fired. Being the youngest waitress at sixteen years of age and in charge of the team, I chose to leave with them so that the restaurant's manager would feel the full impact of not having bus girls. Many of our customers became angry about the quality of service after we left. They quit coming to the restaurant. It closed down in less than three months. I learned very early, even though bosses can be difficult, there are solutions.

Hal DePue
School Superintendent

In 1954 the landmark *Brown vs. Board of Education* Supreme Court decision struck down the policy of white-only and black-only schools all across this land. This meant that no public school could refuse admittance to black students because of where they lived or for any other reason. Many schools did "in fact" have only white students enrolled, in large part because of previously defined school boundary lines. While in his position of Superintendent of the San Mateo Elementary School District from 1964 to 1975, Hal DePue established a policy in 1966 to end *de facto* segregation within the San Mateo school system.

I first met Mr. DePue when I decided to seek employment within the school district. Years earlier I had learned to always go to the top person whenever you want an important decision made. Working with children was important to me, so I decided to go straight to Mr. DePue rather than an office clerk. I can still recall our first conversation:

"I am aware you are the superintendent of the school district," I said matter-of-factly. "The reason I wanted to meet you is to find out if you have any job openings. I'm new in town, I need a job, but I can't take any tests."

"Exactly what do you have in mind?" Hal DePue asked attentively. "I'm curious about not taking any tests. Explain that part."

"While living in San Francisco for the past eight years," I stated, "I took test after test after test. I held many positions as a volunteer and a community leader. It was another whole story when I tried to get a job. I was either not qualified, too old, or had too many kids. I decided no more tests for me."

"How many kids do you have?" Mr. DePue asked.

"Eight," I responded. "I'm good with children and none of my kids have ever been in jail. That ought to count as some qualification to work in the school district."

"Have a seat in my outer office," Mr. DePue said, interested. "I have to make a few calls."

Although I was in the other office, I could partially hear his comments: "I have an interesting woman in my office that might fit in with your need for someone who can handle the overcrowded classes we discussed." Mr. DePue paused. "Well, she has eight children, none have ever been in jail and she definitely likes children." I'm thinking, *I have a lot of nerve. I may never get this job, whatever it is.*

"Mrs. Curry." It was Mr. DePue's voice. "I have good news for you. It might be just what we need to get you started. I have an opening for a Teacher's Aide position. You can see if you like it and work your way up from there." I was speechless.

"Can you start next Monday?" Mr. DePue smiled. "One more thing. No tests," he concluded. We both laughed and shortly thereafter, I began my new job as a Teacher's Aide who took no tests.

James Forrest
Human Relations Director

James Forrest was the Human Relations Director of the San Mateo County Government Center in Redwood City, California, where I was hired to be a Civil Law Investigator. James was responsible for me getting my college degree.

One day he said to me, "A degree is your union card, so arrange your schedule to attend school at night and on Saturdays. It will go faster than you think." The year was 1975.

I immediately enrolled at Antioch West College in San Francisco. I had taken numerous independent study courses and remained an avid reader. More than thirty years after the "Board" man in St. Louis had told the principal I was not college material, I'm ready to go to college. James Forrest was right; the time went by quicker than I could have imagined. I now hold a BA in Human Relations and Creative Arts. The lesson I learned from James Forrest was that whenever another person sees potential in you and gives you good advice, take it and act upon it.

Bill Harrison
Public Affairs Director

At KSOL Radio, Bill Harrison was both News Director and Public Affairs Director prior to my being hired. He became my mentor and taught me the finer points of broadcasting. Bill was a man of integrity and had the utmost patience. I remember, for example, the time when my mind could not comprehend operating one of the many pieces of equipment vital to the 'on-air' work. After a week of me struggling, Bill stopped everything, saying to me, "Okay, whenever your mind goes blank, draw a picture. Today I want you to draw the keyboard. Put every knob and dot in place just as you see it. When you're done, bring it to me." Once I completed the drawing, Bill smiled at me and said, "Remember, whenever you get stuck, stop and draw a picture." I owe my own success at KSOL to the many things I learned from Bill.

Today Bill is employed as an engineer with Occupational Safety CAL-OSHA and lives in Hayward, California with is wife Sandra. They have four adult children and four grandchildren. One of my favorites of Bill's philosophies is "When you run into a mean person, don't get mad or even. Just get out of their way." This philosophy took the Station (and me) a long way.

During my tenure as Public Affairs Director (1978 to 1990) I had the good fortune of working with Bill on a number of assignments. I was responsible for producing and engineering 30-minute weekly on-air talk shows, totaling approximately 1,892 programs over a twelve-year period. My duties covered producing and editing 10,608 public service announcements relevant to the needs of non-profit organizations, maintaining the public files and representing KSOL Radio at various community affairs functions. We produced radio specials on a number of topics and issues, including, *how to Avoid Teen Pregnancies; The AIDS Epidemic; Homelessness; The Life & Work of Dr. Martin Luther King, Jr.; Black Males, an Endangered Species;* and *Women's Issues.*

We were often cited for "Outstanding Community Service." We developed and implemented a unique series of community-based public affairs programs, using a multi-cultural training and broadcasting technique. We trained leaders who were expert in their professional fields to become hosts on the air. The Broadcasters Commission from Houston, Texas honored our program ideas with its prestigious Abe Lincoln National Award for Distinguished Broadcasters in 1980.

Gerald Hroblak
Radio Executive

Gerald Hroblak can best be described as a "Long Distance Boss." A man of quality, he was a master with numbers and a precise accountant long before calculators were in widespread use. He was also tuned into the needs of his employees. Considering he resided in Bethesda, Maryland and those who worked for him lived in several different states, it's a miracle he even knew all of our names. Nevertheless, he was always as close as the telephone and encouraged us to contact him as often we felt the need to. This endeared him to his staff. And creative people, who fascinated him, endeared themselves to him. Once the *Curry Award for Girls and Young Women* was established, Gerry Hroblak became one of its biggest financial supporters.

Ana Navarro
Mediation Administrator

Ana Navarro was the Administrator of the Mediation for San Mateo County in Redwood City. She hired me in 1990 as her assistant. What I viewed as a problem developed immediately. During my first few weeks of employment, Ana did not give me any work to do. When I sought answers, I was told to keep reading the material I had been given. I desperately wanted to do well in this position. But I was getting a bit frustrated with only "reading" assignments.

"Have you ever had any black people work for you before?" I inquired seriously.

"Oh, sure," Ana said swiftly. "It's just that I'm from El Salvador. We are not allowed to tell anyone older than us what to do."

"Ana," I said surprised. "I don't know a thing about mediation. Pretend I'm younger than you, so I can take some of this work off you."

"Okay," she replied, happy and relieved. "I'll have you some work tomorrow morning." Did she ever have me some work to do? Ana and I became Diversity Trainers representing San Mateo County. We held four-hour workshops for more than 2,000 county employees. We were no longer *boss* and *employee*. We became good friends as well. Our friendship carried over beyond the regular job hours. We not only demonstrated Diversity Training strategies; we lived diversity in our daily lives. My life is richer as a result of having had Ana as a magnificent friend.

Ken Shubat
General Manager

From Ken Shubat I learned to be a risk-taker. As the white General Manager of KSOL Radio in San Mateo, California, Ken Shubat was definitely a risk-taker. In the early 1970s he hired a team of black managers (J. J. Jefferies, Program Director; Bill Harrison, News Director; Eleanor Curry, Public Affairs Director; and Sheila Robinson, Gospel Program Director) to manage the day-to-day affairs of KSOL Radio. Competent, we took the station to the top of the charts. KSOL remained in the Bay Area top ten during the turbulent 1970s and all through 1990s. To this day we still hear positive comments about this dynamic team thanks to Ken Shubat's vision and his ability to take risks.

Well Danielle, hopefully this letter has given you a sense of some of the people I have been fortunate enough to meet and in some cases work with.

Love,
Mama Curry

CHAPTER 14

▼

RUNNING WITH
MINISTERS

Dear Danielle

This letter is about the wonderful ministers I have known and the many ways they have helped enrich my life and the lives of countless others.

What is the purpose of people going to the neighborhood church week after week? How about those who attend church services for forty or fifty years? Does a perfect Sunday attendance record make any difference in a person's life? Can you imagine people being transformed from men and women acting out excessive, negative behavior to tranquil human beings with positive behavior? Have you observed people changing after they became a Christian? What exactly does a minister do to help others achieve such transformations? What do you feel after a minister preaches a sermon on Sunday?

Here's how I'd answer these questions. If there were no ministers, there would be no one to christen our babies or baptize us. Ministers want us to visit the sick and care for the unwanted. They do more than perform marriages and officiate at funerals. Ministers' help parents guide their children and teach people how to pray. Did you know how to love your enemies, and encourage your spouse to follow God? What does it mean to demonstrate kindness, keep love alive and promote faith and unity?

Through talking about God, the gospel and his grace, ministers mainly teach us about the Savior, Jesus Christ. We're taught to praise God whether successful or troubled. Finally, ministers walk *with* us and want to save us. All of this amazing spiritual guidance is given to our families from the ministers in our communities. Here are the ministers I have had in my life who have done, or, are doing God's work today.

Reverend Mitchell
Baptist Minister, St. Louis, Missouri

Rev. Mitchell married us on March 22, 1946. During the reception immediately following the ceremony, he came over to us and said the most unusual thing: "Stay out of the white man's prison. It's not any place for children of God. One misstep is easy to get into and hard to get out of."

Rev. Mitchell's advice did not hold significance for me until I witnessed a neighbor's teenage being shot by the police. Since many African American teenage males had collided with the criminal justice system, Rev. Mitchell's words kept us sensitive to such a possibility. We became diligent in our pursuit of keeping our sons out of jail. For example, when our oldest son was ten years old, I went to the police department in San Francisco and spoke to one of the lieutenants on duty. Here's the way the conversation went.

"I want to talk to someone about how to keep our sons from getting shot by the police."

"How old are your sons?" the Lieutenant asked me.

"We have five sons and the oldest is ten. I'm very concerned because one of our neighbor's sons was killed by a police officer last month. I don't want that to happen to any of our sons, so what can we do?"

"Excuse me for a minute," he replied. The he got up and left. A few minutes later the Lieutenant returned and escorted me into Chief Thomas Cahill's office. He warmly greeted me by saying, "What can I do for you, young lady?"

After explaining again why I was there, he said, "I'm glad you came in. We'll see what we can do and get back in touch with you. Within a week Chief Cahill had created the Police Community Relations Unit. He asked me to serve as one of its committee members. We met once a month to discuss how both sides could respect and understand each other. Additionally, uniformed police offices met in some of our homes to discuss safety issues. These discussions helped diminish the fear on the both sides and kept our community safe. The police department was so receptive to our reaching out to them that during the holidays they took up a collection of $500 dollars and gave it to me to share with the neighbors. By the way, none of our sons ended up injured by the police.

Pastor John Richie
Bayview Lutheran Church
San Francisco, California

The most profound affect Pastor John Richie had on our family was when we were all baptized in 1961 in Bayview Hunter's Point. It began with a knock on the door of our home in Hunter's Point. I answered thinking the minister must be lost. Instead of asking for directions, he said to me, "Would you like to come visit our church? It is close by and we are doing outreach missionary recruitment. We hope you will come and join our congregation." We hardly knew anyone except a few neighbors at that time. So we joined Bayview Lutheran Church and entered a world unknown to our family: Volunteerism! We often helped people in our own way, but usually only those in our immediate family. This was different. Suddenly we were helping anybody needing help. We learned from Pastor Richie volunteerism means serving and helping unfortunate people, known and unknown.

Reverend Mary Frazier
Bread of Life Evangelistic Outreach
East Palo Alto, California

I had known Mary for many years prior to her becoming a minister. Previously we had worked together in various school districts when she lived in East Palo Alto, a mostly African American community twenty miles south of San Mateo. One day I opened my mailbox and found a letter with a Tulsa, Oklahoma return address. I was puzzled since I didn't know anyone in Tulsa. The letter read:

Dear Eleanor,

Surprise! Surprise! I have been out of town for a few years studying the ministry. I am now an ordained minister with the Bread of Life Evangelistic Outreach, a non-denominational church. When I return home this summer, I hope we can have lunch, like we have always done.

Looking forward to seeing you soon,

Reverend Frazier

The letter astonished me. I later learned Mary had sold her house after her children had become adults, taken her savings and gone to Tulsa to study for the ministry. She had spent three years towards this endeavor. Upon her return to California, she was officially Rev. Mary Frazier. We met for lunch, catching up on our families and other people we both knew. I asked Rev. Frazier, "Why did you decide to leave your home and become a minister, then return right back to East Palo Alto?"

"I was working at Global Comment as a resource director when I was divinely called by God. I thought that once I finished my studies in Tulsa, I would go to the Caribbean and teach. So I sold my house in Tulsa and came home to East Palo Alto just for a Christmas visit. I decided to stay once again."

Although Rev. Frazier could have served anywhere in the world, including the Caribbean, she chose her former hometown. Once settled, she began a cable TV program entitled *God's Woman*. I asked her, "How did you select the program title *God's Woman?*"

"Several years ago, I had landed an on-air spot at a local community access channel in San Jose. I remember praying to God, asking him, what I should name that program. At that time I was working with a woman named Maureen O'Sullivan. She suggested we call the program *God's Woman*. We were moving tapes swiftly every week so they could be aired. Our program had a major impact and was broadcast weekly for over seven years. So I decided to use that title again. Now I'm producing at the media center in Palo Alto."

"What criteria did you use to select the women for the show?" I asked.

"Women who continue to do His work." Rev. Frazier was excited, moving closer. "They have extraordinary commitment to serving others. They are community oriented. Some of them are ordained, yet few people know this. In fact, very little or any attention is ever paid to these women. They were often awed when I'd call asking them to come and be interviewed."

"Any issues for such women who appear voiceless?" I asked, now keenly involved.

"Gender is the hot button." Rev. Frazier emphatically said. "One of the biggest issues has to do with women in the ministry. They have been licensed and ordained. Most male ministers contend a woman is not called to preach. We reach out to one another, giving moral support, and keep on serving. You see, we don't have any 'Good Old Boys' network. But there's immense denial from most male clergy and among women leaders in some congregations. Several years ago Dr. Thomas Cooper, who is now deceased, wrote a book called *Should Women Be Ordained?* His peers rejected him."

Rev. Mary Frazier is currently on the AIDS Outreach Board in San Mateo and continues to serve as Pastor of *Bread of Life Worship Center* in East Palo Alto.

Reverend Dr. Larry Wayne Ellis
New Pilgrim Baptist Church
San Mateo, California

For hundreds of years many of us have pondered the question: *What does it mean to be human?* We all struggle with the dichotomy of opposites—love and hate, lift up and tear down, good *vs.* evil, hope and despair, truth *vs.* lies. By 1985 I had met a man who appeared to be living a God-revering life-style. Rev. Larry Ellis, minister of Pilgrim Baptist Church in San Mateo, has had a dramatic effect on the lives of many people on a daily basis. We know it is the role of the minister to talk about the Holy Bible. What does this role mean to the minister's own congregation? Rev. Ellis made the minister's role plain with early sermons that focused on love. In his *Message of Spiritual Love*, a particularly profound sermon, Rev. Ellis spoke to us about the "love" side of love *vs.* hate. Here are excerpts from that sermon:

Paul wrote the Letters of Spiritual Love by telling what love truly is— the real understanding of love and how its application is so simple, yet so profound. What does the world need now? It needs love. We do not need any more microscopic studies to pinpoint a fly on the outer rim of space. We do not need any more military build-ups. There are enough houses for every person, enough cars and enough laws. Yet the world is falling apart.

The primacy of love says 'Love thy neighbor as thyself.' The practicality of love is patience, kindness, long suffering, faith, charity and hope, but the greatest being charity. Love is not arrogant, proud, self-seeking, easily provoked, full of evil, not thinking and not rejoicing in sin.

Take your mind out of RUTSVILLE! We stand on God's truth. Cast out fear by practicing love, for perfect love casts out fear. There's no fear in love. Love is fearless, too. Love is always having the other's spiritual best in mind.

When we slip from this attitude, we must ask questions: 'What have we failed to do?' Or, 'Why does love grow cold?' While working on what we have done, and what we can do to return to the heat, we are always in danger of being lukewarm, for this cools love. As Christians we cannot be in a defensive corner, saying, 'I hope they don't bother me.'

We all seek acceptance, appreciation and acknowledgement. We have to prepare ourselves by building our characters, lest we fall fast. We must be courageous, not be 'wishy-washy' in doing what we're commissioned to do. The straight shooting Savior explains it so easily, yet it's so hard to understand. But keep on. Walk down the street called 'Straight', with love, knowing that love bears all things, believes, hopes and endures all things. Love never fails, has a long list of credits, and is permanent. Love is what we are.

*   *   *   *

Rev. Ellis closed this sermon amidst thunderous clapping and shouts of "Amen!" Danielle, Rev. Ellis is a profound teacher, taking his message beyond preaching. His speeches are easy to remember, easy to quote and easy to practice. According to Dr. Ellis, there are five dimensions of a complete life:

1.   Spiritual—Taking responsibilities for the thoughts that come into our head
2.   Relational—the goal is to develop healthy relationships not toxic (harmful)
3.   Center—under control
4.   Financial Stewardship—the three T's:

Time: How you use it, devote to God quality time.

Talent: Do not sit on the gift that God gave you.

Treasure: Do not store treasures for yourself, share with others.

5.   Physical—if the body is the Temple of God, it does matter what you put into it.

Another favorite message for which Rev. Ellis received rave comments concerned his thoughts on one of his favorite anachronisms. Those comments went like this:

The movie industry can teach us much about ministry. The executive producer develops funding. The casting agency selects personnel. The director makes it happen from the first shot to the final cut. There are many 'extras.' In ministry, God is the executive. The Holy Spirit is the casting agency and the Lord directs the 'show.' However, in God's kingdom, there are no 'extras.' Everyone is needed. It is time to hear our Lord cry ACTION!

A   *Accountability: Commitment to mutual responsibility to use your gift, support the ministry and be a team player. (1 John 1:6-10)*

C   *Compassion: Care for others enough to enter their lives and bring the love of God through you. (1 Peter 3:8)*

T   *Togetherness: Living out the Lord's call to be one. (John 17)*

I   *Involved: A desire to get into the "mix" of ministry, not on the sidelines, but in the trenches; using a count me in mentality.*

O   *Open: Many saints seek to live private isolated lives. We can never be whole without being open. We are only as sick as our secrets. (Acts 2:42-47)*

N   *Now: Time is a continuously diminishing resource. Jesus said, 'The day you hear my voice...don't delay. Now is the hour to do ministry.' (1 Peter 5:8-9).*

The director is sounding the call for ACTION! Let those who have ears listen and obey.

*   *   *   *

I hope this gives you a broad picture of how Rev. Ellis' sermons have been a tremendous influence on our daily lives. When I was about nine years old the first scripture I happened to memorize spelled out the word GOSPEL. Here is that verse:

God so loved the world that He gave his
Only begotten Son, that whosoever believes in Him
Shall not
Perish, but have
Everlasting
Life.
(John 3:16)

This has been an incredible writing experience, Danielle. I hope you enjoy it as much as I enjoyed writing it.

Love,
Mama Curry

Epilog

Questions cause us to pause, to seek responses and to share the mystery that dwells in our minds, hearts and souls. Questions break open the vast silence of day-in day-out living. Questions penetrate mental blockage and shake up complacent behavior. Questions bring forth thoughts that matter to others that we are unaware of. Questions challenge behavior, having us look at our actions in situations. Questions help us search to clear up disputes or doubts. Questions speak, saying someone else is watching. Questions rise up to pierce the unconscious mind.

Every answer to every question might sound different, yet every answer seems to eventually pinpoint similar universal truths. These truths, visible and invisible views, constitute life. So when one pauses, thinks about another and tells that person what one is thinking, that's freedom. When one makes planned pauses, too, one makes expressions of freedom. The best of all freedoms is this: *The older we grow/ the more we might know/About God's grace and peace/About God's love/ about love.*

With these thoughts we keep in mind new questions: Can we be open and willing? Can our journey be fulfilling? Is this the best of all possible worlds? Is there a plan that keeps God near? We rest assured, knowing that today God gives us good health; it's better than immense wealth.

Acknowledgments

I am extremely grateful to my husband, *Richmond Earl*, whose willingness to roll up his sleeves and take care of all our household responsibilities enabled me to complete the writing of this book. I want to thank Earl for being a wonderful husband and father to our children for so many years.

I owe a debt of gratitude to three of our adult children, *Bonnie*, *Barbara* and *Bill*. Bonnie was a tremendous resource by bringing her writing and editing skills to this endeavor. In the beginning, I could not have gotten off first base without the help of Barbara. She gave of herself and her time by putting the original draft on a computer. She also revised the material after relentlessly inquiring about the details to help me clarify many of my thoughts. Bill stepped in and kept me informed about how to use the computer. Thanks to him, I was able to gain an understanding of this awesome twenty-first century tool.

I am grateful to *Jill Wakeman-Goodman*, a longtime trusted friend. Jill not only sparked a thirst in me to write, she was tireless in arranging speaking engagements for me so I could promote this book. Frequently she sent me blank journals. Often Jill met with me during the course of this writing giving me the needed encouragement to see it through to the end.

It's easy to get sidetracked especially when working on a major project. Thanks, three times to *Mindy Pengilly*, my son's wife, who on more than one occasion insisted that I stop everything else and just write. Often she would say to me, "Knock off sewing pillows, reading books and going to movies. Just keep writing."

To an incredibly gifted teacher, *Roxanne McDonald*, I must say thanks so much for teaching me the art of memoir writing. This book would not have been possible without her expert guidance.

I discovered the value of a new friend, Laura Teal, a person of many talents. She came on board at the end and helped with some final details. Thanks for caring, Laura.

Last but far from least, I'd like to thank *Danielle* for her inquisitive mind. If she had not asked her questions, I may never have given any thought to writing about family members, many friends and myself.

978-0-595-39513-2
0-595-39513-9

CPSIA information can be obtained
at www.ICGtesting.com
Printed in the USA
LVOW11s2047040417

529585LV00001BA/33/P